BROKEN HALLELUJAHS

BROKEN HALLELUJAHS

WHY POPULAR MUSIC MATTERS
TO THOSE SEEKING GOD

CHRISTIAN SCHAREN

BrazosPress

a division of Baker Publishing Group
Grand Rapids, Michigan

© 2011 by Christian Scharen

Published by Brazos Press
a division of Baker Publishing Group
P.O. Box 6287, Grand Rapids, MI 49516-6287
www.brazospress.com

Printed in the United States of America

Library of Congress Cataloging-in-Publication Data
Scharen, Christian Batalden.
    Broken hallelujahs : why popular music matters to those seeking God /
Christian Scharen.
        p. cm.
    Includes bibliographical references (p.   ) and indexes.
    ISBN 978-1-58743-250-7 (pbk.)
    1. Christianity and culture. 2. Popular culture—Religious aspects—Christianity. 3. Popular music—Religious aspects—Christianity. I. Title.
    BR115.C8S2645 2011
    261–dc23   2011022392

11   12   13   14   15   16   17   7   6   5   4   3   2   1

In keeping with biblical principles of creation stewardship, Baker Publishing Group advocates the responsible use of our natural resources. As a member of the Green Press Initiative, our company uses recycled paper when possible. The text paper of this book is composed in part of post-consumer waste.

to

Timothy F. Lull †

and

Don E. Saliers

The primary impulse of each is to maintain and aggrandize himself. The secondary impulse is to go out of the self, to correct its provincialism and heal its loneliness. In love, in virtue, in pursuit of knowledge, and in the reception of the arts, we are doing this. Obviously this process can be described either as an enlargement or as a temporary annihilation of the self. But that is an old paradox; "he that loseth his life shall save it."

—C. S. Lewis, *An Experiment in Criticism*

He called the crowd with his disciples, and said to them, "If any want to become my followers, let them deny themselves and take up their cross and follow me. For those who want to save their life will lose it, and those who lose their life for my sake, and for the sake of the gospel, will save it."

—Mark 8:34–35

CONTENTS

124119

ACKNOWLEDGMENTS

I had to laugh when I sat down to tackle this last lovely task of giving thanks. I had finished a book on imagination, pop culture, and God, now four years in the making, accruing many debts in that time. The first thing that popped into my head was the last hit single released by ABBA, the Swedish pop foursome, titled "Thank You for the Music." The song is very nearly a prayer and gives heartfelt thanks for the joy that comes from the singing, the songs, and the music. Indeed, to paraphrase their question in the lyric, who *could* live without it? What *would* this life be were we not able to sing and dance? So I begin with thanks to God, whose creative and loving life opened time and space for the creation of the cosmos, for our lives, and for the beautiful gift that is music. As well, thanks for all the musicians and artists whose work blesses my life, stretches my imagination, and tutors me in "the full stretch of living."

I learned that little phrase "the full stretch of living" from Don Saliers, my teacher and mentor while I was in graduate school at Emory University. On his door he had a sign quoting St. Irenaeus of Lyons, who said, "The glory of God is humanity fully alive." Don, a gifted theologian and musician himself, has both jazz and blues in his background as well as classical musical training. With his daughter, Emily (one-half of the folk music duo the Indigo

Girls), Don has lived and written beautifully about the intersections of faith and pop music, sacred and secular. Another teacher and mentor, Tim Lull, who died tragically at age sixty in 2003, regularly engaged with pop culture and music in his teaching, even lecturing in his black boots and leather jacket on days he was attending a rock-and-roll show with one of his sons. To both of these men I owe deep gratitude.

Many other people and places have welcomed me as I thought through these arguments. First, thanks to Barney Cochran and Ron Wright for inviting me to give the "Imagination and the Kingdom of God" lecture at Mount Vernon Nazarene University. Neither you nor I had any idea that your invitation would lead to this book! I hope it comes as a blessing and an encouragement to the vital and faithful work you pursue there.

At Brazos Press, Rodney Clapp believed in my ideas and exercised patience as I dragged the project from New Haven to St. Paul. That move added years to the writing time, no doubt, but as contractual deadlines came and went, Rodney stayed the course. I deeply value his editorial wisdom and sage insights on popular culture. My thanks to the Brazos production and marketing staff as well, especially Lisa Ann Cockrel, whose prodding and questions strengthened the whole book.

Thanks also to Holden Village, Camp Arcadia, the Nebraska Synod (ELCA) and Midland University, the ELCA Youth Extravaganza, and many congregations where I have presented some of these ideas. The long delay in publishing the book is mostly due to my transition from Yale Divinity School and its Center for Faith and Culture to my present position at Luther Seminary. Yet the provocative questions and conversations in these many settings forced new thinking and further work on my part. Thanks to all.

Particular friends and colleagues have offered help and inspired my thinking. To Yale colleagues Miroslav Volf, Carolyn Sharp, Martin Jean, and Siobhan Garrigan (now at the University of Exeter), thank you. To Luther colleagues Eileen Campbell-Reed, Mary Hess, Dirk Lange, David Lose, Andy Root, Dick Nysse, and Dwight Zscheile, along with Dean Roland Martinson, thank you. Teaching alongside you and discussing these and many related issues deepened my work and inspired my writing. Other scattered friends have been key encouragers of this work: the Collegeville

Group (Ted Smith, Dorothy Bass, Bonnie Miller-McLemore, Jim Nieman, Kathleen Cahalan, and John Witvliet), Tom Beaudoin, Pete Ward in the UK, and Alan Storey in South Africa. I am particularly grateful for Ted Smith's invitation to think through the ways particular book projects shape us as persons. I think this book has, more than anything I've written, changed me for the better. Finally, a special thanks to two outstanding research assistants, Jeni Falkman Grangaard and Peter Speiser, whose love of pop music and theology led to many great conversations. Likewise, thanks to Catrina Ciccone, who worked with me on final edits and put together the indexes. I learned from all these colleagues, and the book is much better for their presence in my life.

Last, a brief word of thanks is due to Sonja, my partner and spouse, and my two children, Isaiah and Grace. Actually, no mere word of thanks would do for the ways they have loved me in spite of my many faults. Perhaps the phrase we all learned in Scandinavia during a recent summer trip is better: *tusen takk*. The book not only would have been worse without the joy you bring to my life; it wouldn't have been at all.

PART I

GOD IN POPULAR CULTURE

1

THE SEDUCTIVENESS OF CERTAINTY

Instead, get help from the God of Jacob,
    put your hope in God and know real blessing!
God made sky and soil,
    sea and all the fish in it.

—Psalm 146:5–6

A TALE FROM THE HEARTLAND

I was nervous. It was one of those moments when, no matter the bold claim of my antiperspirant in TV ads, my anxiety overwhelms my shirt. It was clear from the hour's drive through rural towns and country fields, past American flags and Bible-quoting billboards, that rural Ohio was a long way from the ivied halls of New Haven, Connecticut, where I lived and worked at the time. As I walked into the auditorium where I planned to screen and discuss a Kanye West rap video that included a prostitute, a cocaine bust, and little girls singing profanity while they jumped rope, I wished I'd prepared a different lecture.

Inviting me to kick off the "Imagination and the Kingdom of God" speaker series at Mount Vernon Nazarene University, my faculty host Ron Wright had warned me over dinner that the

Christian school leaned strongly toward the conservative evangelical side of the faith. He confided that my invitation was a bit of a risk, inasmuch as my theme–faith and "secular" pop music–would raise eyebrows. Yet as we conversed in his office, he introduced me to *Paste* magazine, whose tagline, "Signs of Life in Music, Film, and Culture," intrigued me. He said the struggle at the university was finding ways to press the narrow bounds of truth and faith out into the complexity of life as we experience it. *Paste* helped him do that.[1]

I had a sense of what Ron was talking about, because I had done some poking around ahead of time. I'd found and read the university's code of Christian conduct (called Lifestyle Guidelines) that all the students, faculty, staff, and administration agree to abide by. While honesty was the cardinal virtue, five specific things received focus: alcohol, drugs, tobacco, sexual promiscuity or harassment, and "inappropriate entertainment." I gathered that the guidelines listed the entertainment item last so it would be clear that the presence of any of the prior four in this or that entertainment form would place it in the "inappropriate" column. *Great*, I thought, *my lecture will pretty much hit all four, and so my contribution to the "Imagination and the Kingdom of God" series will be categorized as "inappropriate entertainment."*

It wasn't as if Mount Vernon Nazarene didn't want their students to be able to listen to hip new tunes. The weekend after my visit, in fact, the university was playing host to an annual rock music festival called SonFest. As in *the* Son, who sitteth at the right hand of the Father, as the Apostles' Creed puts it. The artists and bands playing at SonFest were drawn from the lists of contemporary Christian artists. I, however, was going to argue that that same Son was at the heart of Kanye West's rap songs too, even if he would never make the invitation list for SonFest. I hadn't told my hosts that much about my plans for the lecture and wondered to myself whether I should quickly shift gears and speak about something safer, like U2's song "Beautiful Day," with its biblical background drawn from the prophet Isaiah. That's why they'd invited me, after all; they'd read my book on U2 and the theology of the cross.[2]

However, as I got my laptop set up and experimented with the projection and sound, I struck up a conversation with the students running the soundboard. They saw that I was going to talk about

Kanye West, and with a slight glance around, as if perhaps someone was watching, they turned up the music's volume on their control-room speakers. The unmistakable techno beat nicked from Daft Punk filled the room, followed by the unmistakably cocky lyrics of the hit single "Stronger": "na, na, na that that don't kill me, can only make me stronger." The song was from Kanye West's 2006 album *Graduation*, an album that had sold over a million copies since its release two weeks prior. As their heads bobbed to the beat, they told me that students would be with me, eager to talk about this music in relation to their faith. They assured me it was widely enjoyed, if with some guilt.

By the appointed hour, the auditorium was packed, and I launched into my lecture. I went on a bit longer than I'd planned. Still, the question-and-answer period easily went longer than the fifty-minute lecture, as the students and faculty who had gathered joined me in vibrant engagement with the big question I'd raised at the outset: how can we find a faith-filled imagination deep and substantial enough for the struggles we face in this time? This book is, in large part, a continuation and deepening of that night's conversation.

What are the struggles we face today? Some of the "century" challenges we face—including climate change, conflicts of religion and identity, shortages of oil, water, and food—all require a renewed imagination to find not only solutions but also the calling to join in the work of love and justice that can accomplish them. This book emerges from my conviction that we desperately need imagination that looks the brokenness of humanity and the groaning of creation straight in the face but that also knows mercy and reconciliation have been offered by God in Christ, who through the Holy Spirit is working in the midst of all our sorrows even now. This mercy is the first and final word, our promised future, and the ground of our present possibilities. Christians ought to stake their lives upon this promise. Further, they ought to build their cooperation with others upon such a promise. The question at the heart of this book is how to find—or better yet, how we are found by—a God of promise and mercy who offers all of us an imagination deep and substantial enough for the struggles the world faces in our day.

"Well," some might argue, "don't we already have all the imagi-native resources we need?" It is true that in many senses our time is exploding with imagination. We could think of the medical imagination that has created such a wide array of options to limit the burden of illness in our lives. We could think of the technological and scientific imagination that has allowed us to explore the vastness of space as well as the basic building blocks of life. We could continue the litany, in full knowledge that these kinds of imagination have sometimes been used to horrible ends—atomic and biological weapons, for instance—but nonetheless confident that we are much better off in the world for having such imagination and its many results. In fact, those visions of possibility and creativity are gifts of a boundlessly creative God from whom all blessings flow, through our bodies and minds, into the life of the world.

GETTING OVER CERTAINTY [3]

Yet, in relation to faith, we too often take the outpouring of God's superabundance, like the mountain waterfall in spring thundering over cliffs to the river below, and we bottle it, saying, "Here! We've got it." This book engages the space of interaction between faith and popular culture, especially through popular music, as a case study in this larger challenge of Christian imagination that can meet the challenges we face today.[4] Dominant views on faith and culture too often fit a perspective like the one at Mount Vernon, where a "checklist Christianity" looks skeptically at pop culture for any number of things that would justify its rejection as unworthy. Such narrowing of what can be considered "worthy" cultural objects, works of art that really show us God's glory, subtly tutors us in a constricted imagination that then influences how we engage politics, the environment, economics, science—in short, how we engage all of life.

Constricted Imagination

While there are undoubtedly multiple versions of what I am calling "constricted imagination" active in religions generally and Christianity in particular, this book is an extended conversation with one form that I'm calling "checklist Christianity."[5] This form is a way of embodying the faith that finds its home and most ardent support in conservative evangelical institutions such as Focus on the

Family (whose work at the intersection of faith and pop culture is the subject of chapter 5). Yet the impulse for purity is deep in Christian history, part of a reforming trajectory that connects historically with the ancient priestly role in calling the people of God to holiness (cf. Exod. 19:6; 1 Pet. 2:9). Historian Randall Balmer shows how the intermingling of Puritan and Pietistic influences in America set in motion a particular version of Christianity that highlighted "the necessity of rebirth and the demands for upright living."[6]

Beginning this book by recounting my lecture in Ohio, I am portraying one instance of how we Christians can become captive to a kind of constricted imagination. I will likely not get much resistance on whether or not Christians sometimes suffer from constricted imagination. Certainly my hosts at Mount Vernon Nazarene University saw the limits of such constriction—and engaged in vital discussion with me about ways to stretch our imagination toward God's. They could see the ways such constricted imagination ties us to a dualistic framework for engaging popular culture. Checklist Christianity is, I will argue, a major way that Christians get off track in seeking to foster a faithful imagination, an imagination serious and capacious enough to enlarge our witness in the midst of the troubles of our times.

Glory and the Cross

This book develops and deepens themes I first raised in my book on U2, *One Step Closer*. Of course, one need not read *One Step Closer* to engage this book; each stands on its own terms. Yet here I'd like to say a bit about how *Broken Hallelujahs* emerged as a way to frame some of the key issues that arose in writing and speaking about *One Step Closer*. I wrote *One Step Closer* to help young people see how one band sings of the pressing issues of our day from the perspective of an imagination forged in the fire of faith. U2 have dealt with issues of war, poverty, and ecological crisis again and again in both their art and their advocacy for justice. The band has inspired generations of people to seek God and to join in God's work of mercy and justice in the world. They are, I believe, one of the most important rock bands ever, a fact made more intriguing given that the work and lives of its members are deeply shaped by Christian faith.

Unfortunately, while my work sparked some to engage more deeply with this side of U2, for others my book served to rekindle a debate about whether U2 are lost or found, edifying or dangerous for Christian ears. It was, in my framing of the issue, a version of checklist Christianity holding a ruler up to U2. Here is a version of that issue, raised in an interview with a Christianbook.com editor:

> Editor: In chapter 8 of your book, you call attention to a larger group of Christians (dubbed "Squeakers" by U2) who were very critical of the band's departure from the [Christian] outspokenness of their first two albums. Thus, many evangelical Christians saw the era between *The Joshua Tree* [1987] and *Pop* [1997] as a period in which U2 had presumably fallen from their faith. Why do you think so many were drawn to this misunderstood conclusion? . . . What I find almost more interesting is how quickly evangelical Christians reattached themselves to U2 once *All That You Can't Leave Behind* was released in 2000, especially those who had once written them off as lost. What is your take on this sudden reattachment, and do you believe this return to overt spirituality was an intentional effort to recapture this audience?[7]

I responded to the question by drawing on a main theme of that book: comparing the theology of glory to the theology of the cross.[8] I said that "squeakers" believe in glory, not the cross. Both the theology of glory and the theology of the cross are coherent theologies that begin with varying understandings of human beings. The theology of glory understands sin as a minor defect. Sin simply makes us predisposed to act badly. Thus, we are optimistic that with a little energy boost from Christ—as if he's a can of energy drink—we can be who God expects us to be and thereby have certainty that we are blessed.

The theology of the cross sees sin as something wrong at our core, something we cannot overcome alone. We stumble, but on account of Christ we have hope. We are joined to his death and resurrection, dying to sin and being made alive in Christ. So we have faith that God's mercy covers our fault and speak of the cross as sufficient for our salvation. Tellingly, Bono draws on Philip Yancey's lovely book *What's So Amazing about Grace?* to lament the fact that so many Christians think their "good" behavior will earn them passage through the pearly gates of heaven.[9] Instead, with Yancey,

Bono can argue that it's "who you know that gets you through" despite your unworthiness.[10]

What I tried to make clear to the Christianbook.com editor, and to others who asked similar questions, is this: I don't think the U2 of the 2000s made a play to overt faith to regain an audience they had lost in their period of "wandering" in the 1990s. In the opinion of the band, overt faith was present all the way through. The issue turns out to be the *way* faith was overt. Unfortunately, U2 lost an audience among some Christians during the late 1980s and 1990s as a direct result of a faulty theology that says, "If you admit doubt, your faith is not strong enough, and you are in spiritual peril." See how it starts with an "if"? The theology of glory says our relationship to God depends on us; it is an if/then proposition. One might summarize it as, "If you do good, then God gives good to you (and vice versa)." The summary version of the theology of the cross says our relationship to God depends on God; it is a because/therefore proposition. One might summarize it as "[Because] Christ died 'for us,' therefore God shows us unconditional love, forgiveness, and mercy." The theology of glory is in some sense predictable and amounts to an unremarkable extension of standard human expectation onto our image of God. The theology of the cross, however, is surprising and scandalous by human standards–only a merciful and loving God would have thought it up for us.[11]

So, the theology of glory leads with an "if" perspective: *if* U2 are explicit enough about their faith, then Christians should listen. *If* they are explicit about their doubt, then Christians beware–that's a sign they are losing their way, and in following you just might lose your way as well. From this perspective, U2's smash hit of 1987 "I Still Haven't Found What I'm Looking For" began the band's public departure from orthodox faith. Such a perspective misunderstands both U2 and God. That is a strong statement, but I have reasons for making it that I will outline here, before stepping back to more fully develop my position.

Grace Makes Beauty Out of Ugly Things

There is no truly or completely "secular" culture or arena of human life if you believe that God is Creator of heaven and earth, the seas and all that is in them (Ps. 146:6; Acts 14:15). When Jesus says that God makes it rain on the just and the unjust (Matt. 5:45), he is saying something profound in relation to how we regard popular culture. Take, for instance, *Walk the Line*, a movie about Johnny Cash and June Carter. It is a complex story, including deep suffering, drug addiction, divorce, and also great love, repentance, and healing. Ultimately, it is a story about how, in the words of U2, God's grace "makes beauty out of ugly things." Cash's life was "covered" by a mercy greater than all his troubles.[12] The question arises in the context of this discussion: was God present only in Cash's "gospel" songs, or was God also present when Cash sang "Folsom Prison Blues" to a room full of prisoners?[13]

U2 present us with this challenge. While meeting with religion reporters after his "homily" at the National Prayer Breakfast in 2006, Bono said, "I'm asked, 'Why doesn't your music proclaim Christ?' and my answer is that it does." He went on say, "Creation has its own proclamation of God. I'd like to think our music has the same qualities to it."[14] Can the church find a profound-enough view of sin to see its own faults, and can it find a profound-enough view of creation and grace to see God's presence working in the world? U2 might ask us this: do we proclaim God only when we sing about divine love in the songs "Gloria" or "Grace," or do we proclaim God also when we sing about human love in the songs "Desire" and "Discothèque"? If we split culture dualistically, with sacred on one side and secular on the other, we risk missing the very human presence in "Gloria" and "Grace," and the heavenly resonances in "Desire" and "Discothèque." More importantly, our imagination is constrained by a shrunken view of the scope of God's domain.[15]

GENRE AND OUTLINE

U2 have always been about holding things in tension–earth and heaven, spirituality and sexuality, faith and doubt. At root, as they see it, the issue is a theological one, an issue about being true to who God is and who we are created to be. Inspired by this challenge, this book has two things at its heart. First is to have a go at writing a sound biblical theology for engaging popular culture. Enough of the theology of constricted imaginations! We need to recover a vibrant and imaginative theology of grace that can orient Christian living in these times. Second is getting a sound method for engaging the voices of popular culture where God is already at work reconciling the lost, healing the broken, and speaking the truth of life. Of course, there is much to object to in popular culture, but if we have our theology straight, we know there is as much to object to in the church, and in our own hearts as well. The key question we have to ask ourselves is whether we shall try to hole up and save our life only to lose it or venture out to lay down our lives, that we might be surprised by a mercy that saves us (Mark 8:35).

Before turning to the movement of the chapters that lie ahead, I want to offer two ways that might help make sense of the genre of this book. First, I borrow from the novelist Barbara Kingsolver, especially *The Poisonwood Bible*, her powerful tale of colonial missions in the Congo. From this book I learned the idea of trying to get at the same moment or element from various angles of vision. In *The Poisonwood Bible* the same scene is replayed in sequential chapters through the perception of various characters: the mother, a daughter, and so on. I adopt that approach here, trying to get at a common scene–the paradoxical nature of human hope and despair, joy and suffering, and the ways God is revealed in the midst of it all–from various points of view, including Leonard Cohen, the blues, and Scripture. The paradoxical nature of our lives before God is ultimately revealed most fully in Jesus, the crucified and risen one.

Second, borrowing from Nicholas Healy's fine theological work *Church, World and the Christian Life*, I employ the idea of a cumulative argument. Were you to decide not to read from chapter 1 straight through chapter 7, you would be rewarded in many particular ways, but the sense of my overarching argument would elude you. So I encourage both reading straight through and withholding judgment about whether the book makes any sense until the end. It is, as you will see, a strategy I recommend for reading any book, listening to any song, or watching any film.

Broken Hallelujahs is written in two parts. Part 1, "God in Popular Culture," portrays the difficulties of a theology of culture based upon checklist Christianity and the constricted imagination it fosters. Beginning in chapter 2 with the work of singer-poet Leonard

Cohen, I ask how we might articulate a theology of culture that calls us to trust God's presence in the midst of a broken creation, listening to its cries, and ultimately dying for the sake of those cries, working reconciliation that offers a promised new day of shalom for all. Chapter 3 engages blues music in order to further unpack the same question of how to articulate a theology of culture that can look suffering and brokenness in the face because it knows of a love deeper than hate, a hope stronger than despair. I complicate the notion that the blues is the devil's music, drawing a parallel between its moans and cries of lament and those laments in Scripture. Chapter 4 takes these questions up a third time, offering the perspective of cries in Scripture and God's response as another way to help articulate this theology of culture I'm laboring to articulate layer by layer, chapter by chapter.

In part 2, Popular Culture in God, I turn to ask what sort of theology allows us to acknowledge and live in proximity to the cries of suffering in the world. Chapter 5 engages in an extended case study of one prominent example of a theology of culture I view as problematic: that undergirding the work of Dr. James Dobson's organization, Focus on the Family, and its popular media publication *Plugged In*. While I appreciate and share its concern with the cries of suffering in the world, I show how its very means of response keeps it from joining God's mercy and justice already present in even the darkest spaces of abandonment. Chapter 6 draws deeply from the work of C. S. Lewis to make another way altogether, a way Lewis terms a *via crucis*. Lewis will be an unlikely place from which to develop a theology of popular culture in a "minor key," as I have described the theology of the cross.[16] Yet Lewis's own life of suffering and joy makes him a particularly authentic and compelling voice to guide us as we seek to make sense of this crazy earthly life, lived before God and our neighbor.

In the final chapter, I work from the theology of culture developed in the book to offer a series of evocative case studies engaging pop culture. In the book's main body, I engage representatives from musical genres as diverse as folk, rock, jazz, blues, and hip-hop in some depth. In this final chapter, in addition to a brief discussion of the Harry Potter series (books and films), I engage two interesting bands–Sigur Rós and Arcade Fire–that fit within avant-garde genres some have labeled both "postrock" *and* "postclassical." I could add many more, but these few additional minicases are the beginning of a study guide for groups who wish to pursue this conversation in relation to their own set of pop culture associations, on TV, at the movies, on iTunes, or whatever else our imaginations create. The study guide and accompanying videos will be available free of charge on my website, www.christianscharen.com/broken-hallelujahs.html. Music–and various other sorts of popular arts–forms our imagination, enlarging our awareness of the work of reconciliation God is always already in the midst of. God calls us to join in as broken-but-beginning-to-be-healed coconspirators in the great unfolding of our lives in God.

2

THE HOLY AND THE BROKEN
HALLELUJAH

Hallelujah! O my soul, praise God!
All my life long I'll praise God,
singing songs to my God as long as I live.

—Psalm 146:1–2

BOOGIE STREET

In early 2007, Terry Gross, the host of the popular NPR show *Fresh
Air*, interviewed Leonard Cohen. He had recently left the Mount
Baldy Zen Center in Los Angeles, where he had spent the previous
five years. With a new album, *Ten New Songs*, and a book of poems,
Book of Longing, recently released, Cohen's now fifty-year career
seemed surprisingly vital. It needed to be vital. During his years at
Mount Baldy, his accountant had made merry with Cohen's money.
A lawsuit was in process, but Cohen was nearly broke.

Realizing this fact, and curious about the phrase "Boogie Street"
that appeared in his new poems and songs, Gross began by having
Cohen read a poem including the phrase.[1] After he finished the

lines, she asked him: "What does 'Boogie Street' mean to you?" His response was instructive. *Boogie Street* is a way to describe our lives. We're hustling, working, trying to make it from day to day. "We believe that we leave it from time to time, we go up a mountain or into a hole, but most of the time, we're hustling on Boogie Street one way or another."[2]

Intrigued by Cohen's five-year hiatus in the Zen Center, Terry Gross asked about his own trip "up a mountain," wondering aloud whether that served as a retreat from Boogie Street. Gross knew of Cohen's well-documented struggles with depression and perhaps imagined that his famously dark songwriting, grappling with the world's troubles and his own, might have found some relief, an enlightenment of sorts, through escaping the world. Hardly, Cohen responded. "Actually," he said, "a monastery is just part of Boogie Street."

> In fact, on Boogie Street you go back to your flat or your apartment and you close the door and you kind of eliminate the rest of the world, you kind of eliminate Boogie Street. So, there's really more respite from Boogie Street on Boogie Street than there is in a monastery because a monastery is designed to eliminate private space. There's a saying–"like pebbles in a bag the monks polish one another." So in that kind of situation you are always coming up against someone else. So in a certain sense coming up against someone else all the time is Boogie Street.

The parable of the stones polishing one another represents in part Cohen's need for discipline and routine. He has always lived a monastic life of sorts. He rises early in the morning to write, committed to sitting at his desk for those hours of the day's dawning. Interviewers often note with surprise the very Spartan surroundings of his various flats and houses. Yet the particular sort of boogie street, the particular polishing, that the monastery offered allowed a kind of peace to come over his life that had eluded him through decades of suffering and depression. It was not in a moment, but gradually, that he felt a certain sweetness seep into his daily routine.

While his "enlightenment," as some have called it, came through Zen practice, Zen never became his religion. Throughout his life Cohen has remained deeply connected to Judaism. His fight with God over the trials of this life always came rather naturally to him.

It was his need to let go of the fight that he found in Zen practice. It offered him a disciplined space for emptying the self. Cohen describes it this way:

> In one of these dreary Zen meditation halls it is a Zen practice to invite you to sit motionless for long hours, with an officer patrolling the meditation hall to strike you with a stick several times on each shoulder if you nod off. If you sit there long enough, you run through all the alternative ways the events in your life could have turned out. After a while, the activity of thinking, that interior chatter, begins to subside from time to time. And what rushes in, in the same way that light rushes into a room when you switch on the light, is another kind of mood that overtakes you.[3]

A line from his song "The Anthem" portrays this fault line in Cohen's life. There are cracks, Cohen croons, "in everything–that's how the light gets in."[4] His wisdom about the brokenness of life allowed him maturity in his Zen practice, a kind of modest seeking; he acknowledged that above all he simply needed to let go. The light, however, might more accurately be described as emanating from the one he calls "G-d," a way of naming the holy that even in its writing inscribes modesty about the Name revealed in the burning bush in Exodus 3.

Throughout his life Leonard Cohen has sought to understand the full stretch of living in relation to the holy. This search, while inquiring into many other traditions, has centered on the deep tidal pull of the ritual and roots of Judaism. Cohen has remained a Jew throughout his life, and many of his most moving songs and poems call to mind that at the heart of his struggle is a struggle with God. In one short poem in *The Book of Longing*, referring to Mother Teresa's journals, in which she expressed her own deep doubts, he quips: "G-d bless her for letting us know / That she couldn't take it either."[5]

Yet his doubts about God, the world, and his own life meet God's call in ways he seems unable to resist. In another poem, Cohen laments that his time is running out and still he has "not sung the true song, the great song." One can almost hear him in the closing of the poem mumbling his question half resentfully, half gratefully, asking, "Why do you lean me here / "Lord of my life / lean me at this table / in the middle of the night / wondering / how to be beautiful."[6]

One of the greatest songwriters of our time who thinks he hasn't sung the true song, the great song. A consummate ladies' man that nonetheless claims to have spent most nights alone. A man referred to as the "poet laureate of pessimism" whose most famous song raises songs of praise to the Lord of Song. The contradictions and paradoxes unfold like the twisting, turning, unfolding petals on the gardenia flower, a favorite of Cohen from his years living on the Greek island of Hydra. The "flower" of Cohen's life is all the more beautiful for the way it has bloomed so fully, honestly, and fragrantly.

My engagement with the life and art of Leonard Cohen offers not just an overall theme for this book but also its deep structure, not in the simplistic sense that I slavishly follow his ideas but in the sense that he offers a key example, a first flower in the bouquet, if you will, that shows us the complexity and beauty to be found at the intersection of imagination, pop culture, and God. While this chapter focuses on one flower, the rest of the book could be seen as filling out the bouquet. The image of a flower and a bouquet lead me to the analogy of a garden. Imagine Cohen's life and art as a beautiful, sweet gardenia we find in the garden. What needs to be told here to describe the garden, and the beautiful white flower we have before us? First, I'll tell you the story about how the flower grew, and its place in the garden. Cohen's whole life can't be told here, so selection is necessary and focused on supporting my overall interests and focus. Second, however, I'll focus in on the one flower, seeking to understand something of the mysterious and compelling scent at the heart of the flower. In the case of Cohen's life and art, this "scent" centers in his mid-1980s album *Various Positions* and a companion volume of poetry, *Book of Mercy*. Looking closely at these in tandem will help to focus our attention on the elements of Cohen's work that, like the beautiful scent of the gardenia, work to attract generation after generation of admirers.

GROWING

Growing up in a well-to-do Jewish enclave in Montreal, Leonard Cohen's early years were shaped by the intersection of home, school, and synagogue. His father, Nathan, was a third-generation Montreal Jew, working in the family clothing business that had placed them in the upper echelons of social life. His mother, who had escaped Lithuanian pogroms as a child, came from a family of scholars and was fond of singing the folk songs from her childhood around the house. Cohen remembers the ordering patterns of Friday night Shabbat and the singing in the synagogue, its ritual patterns and songs influencing his life and music for decades to come.

The happy home life was broken in 1947 with the illness and subsequent death of his father, Nathan. Leonard was only nine years old, and one way to read the story of his life is as a search for father figures, beginning with his maternal grandfather, Rabbi Klein. Young Leonard would sit for long hours by his grandfather's side studying the Torah and the prophets, especially Isaiah. Cohen recalls it was not his desire to become a biblical scholar like his grandfather but rather that he was "interested in Isaiah for the poetry,"[7] as well as the fiery prophetic vision.

When he was still in high school, Leonard bought a used guitar and began to learn folk songs, influenced partly by his mother's love of traditional music and partly by friends with whom he attended a summer camp. Cohen's infatuation with music continued when he began university at McGill at age seventeen. His second summer there, Cohen and two friends formed the country and western group The Buckskin Boys, wearing buckskin jackets from their fathers' closets. They played dances and parties, and the group lasted throughout his college years, exploring the range of songs gathered in *The People's Songbook*, a collection Cohen received from a summer-camp director.

Cohen discovered a love for poetry in high school, when he chanced across the work of Federico Garcia Lorca's *Selected Poems*. He fell in love with the poet's sensuality and sense of longing. In college he found lifelong poetry mentors and friends in his teachers Louis Dudek and, especially, Irving Layton. Cohen won an undergraduate poetry contest and found himself drawn into the world of words, meter, and rhyme. He fell into a poetry circle, enjoying the work of writing and gathering to critique one another's work, a time he recalls as "an unstructured life; but a consecrated one; some kind of calling."[8] It was this group that midwifed Cohen through the publication of his first collection of poems, *Let Us Compare Mythologies*, bringing together work written between age fifteen, when he discovered Lorca, and the end of college at age twenty-one. He dedicated the book to Dudek.

During these years Cohen first began to feel the effects of what would be a decades-long struggle with depression. The growing feeling of isolation, of being an outsider in his hometown, led him to New York for graduate work in English at Columbia. While he hated the dryness of the studies, he found the lively beat scene there fascinating and drank deeply from its wells of creative inspiration. Here he first experimented with putting poetry to music, although in the mode of jazz poetry readings, something he continued when he returned to Montreal to write. Soon, Cohen sent his publisher the manuscript of a second book of poems, *Spice Box of Earth*. (The evocative title is drawn from the box that is blessed and then its contents inhaled after sundown on the Sabbath, marking the boundary between the sacred and the profane.) Soon after, with the help of a Canadian Arts Council grant, he traveled to London and then to the Greek island of Hydra, where he bought a house and settled among a small expatriate community of writers. Alternately fasting and taking drugs to aid his concentration and imagination, falling in and out of love with the first important woman in his life, Marianne Ihlen, Cohen wrote another book of poetry and two novels. These were critical successes, but none offered the kind of sales that would sustain a life as a writer.

In 1966, back in Montreal, Cohen introduced his literary circle to the work of Bob Dylan and announced that he would become the Canadian version of Dylan. After a short, failed stint exploring country music in Nashville, Cohen returned to New York. He caught hold of the winds blowing through the folk music revival, then in full swing, and took up residence at the famed Chelsea Hotel with the likes of Dylan, Joan Baez, Judy Collins, Allen Ginsberg, Kris Kristofferson, and Janis Joplin. He played a few of his songs for Judy Collins, who asked him to keep in touch. Back in Montreal, he wrote his famous song "Suzanne" and phoned Judy Collins. She loved it, put it on her next album, and invited him back to New York to play in concert with her. His first album, *Songs of Leonard Cohen*, appeared a year later.

While caught up in the New York folk scene, Cohen always had a troubled relationship with its prophetic intentions and was a reluctant bearer of the mantle "spokesperson for the generation" that was foisted upon him. The prophetic tradition and, as I said above, especially Isaiah made a deep impression on Cohen. In an early 1960s lecture at a symposium on the future of Judaism in Canada titled "Loneliness and History," Cohen lamented the collapse of the prophet–priest tension into the priestly alone within his experience of middle-class Jewish culture.[9] Whereas the priest tended the internal well-being of the community, the prophet spoke over against the community, calling it to account for its complicity with injustice. What had been a spiritual and prophetic religious tradition had, Cohen argued, become superficial and material, concerned with the nominal survival of the group rather than with the survival of their role as witnesses to God.[10]

Even as Cohen acknowledged the need for a renewed prophetic voice, he did not claim a position of righteous judgment. Famously, he traveled to Havana in 1961–not out of solidarity with the people but for adventure, to see for himself "what it really meant for men to carry arms and kill other men."[11] American Communists in Cuba denounced him as a "bourgeois individualist"; it was true, after all, that his family owned a clothing factory! He came away from the trip decidedly against the sort of repression and collectivism Cuba had come to represent.

This ambiguous commitment to the prophetic voice emerged early in Cohen's recorded work. His second album, *Songs from a Room* (1969), offers an example. The second track, titled "Story of Isaac," has biblical roots and contemporary relevance aimed at exposing not just the folly of one side but the folly of both. The song's first two verses are told from the perspective of a nine-year-old Isaac, recounting the story from Genesis 22:1–24. It is chilling to read, as Abraham stands tall above Isaac, eyes shining blue, his cold voice speaking of the vision he must obey. As the third verse begins, the narrator addresses the listener as the "Abraham" of today, the one who builds altars to sacrifice children, and Cohen calls for this to stop. Here, decrying the planners of war who stand with bloody hatchets in their hands, Cohen borders on joining in solidarity with the growing antiwar movement. But in verse four, he warns the antiwar marchers not to call him "brother" too quickly, because he and they also have the lust for blood within them. The song ends with a cry for mercy upon "our" uniforms, either of peace or of war, that we show off like strutting peacocks.

Songs from a Room, recorded in Nashville, established for Cohen a pattern of recording and touring that lasted through the next decades. During his years living in Nashville, Cohen was invited to Los Angeles for the wedding of Steve Stanfield, an old friend from Hydra. Stanfield had turned from drugs to the austere life of Zen practice under the watch of a Japanese Zen Buddhist missionary, Joshu Sasaki Roshi. Cohen had heard about Roshi when Stanfield visited him in New York a few years prior and was moved by the old master's calm demeanor. Cohen left the wedding intrigued, and just a couple of years later he went to visit Roshi at the newly established Mount Baldy Zen Center in the San Gabriel Mountains north of LA. Though he lasted only weeks that time ("walking around in the snow at 3:00 a.m. in sandals," as he later described it), he was drawn in. Over the next several years his relationship with Roshi deepened, and Cohen spent a period as Roshi's secretary, traveling with him to various Trappist monasteries, curious about the connections between these two monastic traditions.

As the 1970s drew to a close, Cohen struggled both personally and professionally. His ten-year partnership with Suzanne Elrod finally ended when she left for France with their two children, Adam and Lorca. While his 1976 album *The Best of Leonard Cohen* was well received in Europe, his star had fallen in the US. If a "best of" album and tour didn't signal the end for Cohen's singing career, his next misadventure would–a shared album produced by legendary, eccentric, and, even then, highly dangerous Phil Spector. At one point in the recording at Spector's mansion, the producer put a gun to Cohen's neck and said, "I love you, Leonard." Cohen replied, "I hope you love me, Phil."[12] The product of their partnership, *The Death of a Ladies' Man* (1977), was panned by critics and ignored by most fans, and Cohen has rarely played any of the songs from the album in concert.

Depressed, he continued to seek respite in the discipline and routine of Mount Baldy as well as in the teaching of Roshi, but an injury to his knee prevented him from continuing Zazen (seated meditation, a core practice in Zen Buddhism). Increasingly traveling between LA, Montreal, and Europe (where Suzanne and the children lived), he renewed his study of Jewish sources and spiritual practices. He prayed daily, studied the Talmud (which he carried with him everywhere), and made contact with rabbis who might help instruct him. Ironically, his study with Roshi opened him to new insights into his own faith: "I came upon texts and attitudes that I wouldn't have been able to understand if I hadn't studied with my old Japanese teacher."[13] This study led into the remarkable midlife achievement of his most spiritual album, *Various Positions* (1984), and a moving volume titled *Book of Mercy*, a collection of fifty prayers. Since I have dedicated a section of the chapter below to discussing these works, I will pass them by here without further comment.

While studying Zen gave Cohen deeper insight for his renewed study of Judaism in the 1980s, that very renewed study led him to finally accept Roshi's invitation to move to Mount Baldy for an extended time, a move that took place in the early 1990s. By this time Cohen had turned sixty, noting his aging in his well-known "Tower of Song," from the 1988 *I'm Your Man*, which famously complains of aching in the places where he once played. (The song also claims that he was born to sing, that he "had no choice," as he was "born with the gift of a golden voice." It's a humorous assertion given his famously depressing monotone voice.) On Mount Baldy he lived in a two-room cabin, eating, meditating, and studying with the monks. He went through the required training to formally become a monk and served as the cook and assistant for Roshi. They also drank a lot, Roshi introducing Cohen to sake, and Cohen in turn sharing his love of red wine. "With him," Cohen reports, "there's no sense of piety divorced from the human predicament."[14]

Nonetheless, the incredibly challenging discipline of the monks' daily schedule was a key element of its attraction for Cohen. He once commented that Zen has

> a kind of empty quality. There is no prayerful worship. There's no supplication, there's no dogma, there's no theology. I can't even locate what they're talking about most of the time. But it does give you an opportunity, a kind of version of Hemingway's "A Clean Well-Lighted Place." It gives you a place to sit that is quiet in which you can work these matters out.[15]

Cohen was not, he often repeats, "looking for a new religion" and insists his own religion is "just fine."[16] He found in his diminutive Zen master a deep calm, a peace, and a strange wisdom that he found irresistible. Yet he notes that he was attracted to more than Roshi's personal charisma. He found clarity in the simple yet rigorous meditation practices that in some ways were the opposite of the elaborate theology and practice of Judaism. It was, as he says, not simply finding a quiet place to sit but the whole routine that worked its powerful effect upon him. (See daily schedule below.)

• 3:00 a.m. wake up	• 12:00 lunch
• 3:10 formal tea	• 12:30 work period
• 3:30 chanting	• 12:40 break
• 4:30–6:30 zazen/ sanzen	• 12:50–2:30 zazen and showers
• 6:45 breakfast	• 2:45 chanting
• 7:20 break	• 3:45–5:30 zazen, sanzen
• 7:30 zazen (meditation)	• 5:45 dinner
• 8:30 teisho (lecture)	• 6:20 break
• 9:45-11:45 zazen (guided meditation)	• 6:30 gyodo (walking/chanting)
• 10:00–11:45 sanzen	• 7:00–9:00 zazen, sanzen

By the time Cohen left for his extended stay at Mount Baldy, he had enjoyed revived fortunes with his audiences. Several factors contributed to these revived fortunes. First, his former backup singer Jennifer Warnes recorded an album of covers titled *Famous Blue Raincoat*, the title of an early 1970s Cohen song. Second, *Tower of Song*, a 1995 tribute album, featured stars such as Bono, Suzanne Vega, Billy Joel, Trisha Yearwood, Elton John, and Willie Nelson. Third, a decade later, a tribute film was released that included concert footage from a tribute show in Australia, intimate interviews with the singers about Cohen, and interviews with Cohen himself. In the film, titled *Leonard Cohen: I'm Your Man*, U2 guitarist Dave Evans, know as "The Edge," sums up his admiration in this way.

> In the early days of Christianity in Ireland some people would wall themselves away from society in caves, thinking that if they separated themselves from the world they would be able to hear God more clearly. Leonard has been like that, going off to get God's words and then bringing them back to the people.[17]

In a sense this was true, but not perhaps in the romantic way The Edge imagined. While Cohen would have liked God to simply hand him songs fully formed, he recalls that "Sisters of Mercy" was "the only time a song has ever been given to me without my having to sweat over every word."[18] Cohen quipped, "If I knew where the good songs came from, I'd go there more often!"[19] Cohen again and again retreated to solitude and the discipline of writing, finding especially important places of escape on Hydra and at Mount Baldy. There he could rise early in the morning to sit and write, disciplined and yet waiting "until something arises that is better than me. Better than my thought. Better than my conception."[20]

A new generation of performers who admire Cohen's work and have made hits out of his songs undoubtedly paved the way for the honors that began to roll in—he was made a Companion of the Order of Canada, the highest civilian award, in 2003 and was inducted into the Rock and Roll Hall of Fame in 2008. This climate of renewed enthusiasm for Cohen's work also warmed popular reception of his album *Ten New Songs* (2001), released a year after leaving Mount Baldy; his subsequent release of a collection of poems and drawings titled *Book of Longing* (2006); and his acclaimed 2008–2010 world tour, the first in fifteen years, resulting in a DVD and CD recording, *Live in London*. His songs have now been covered literally thousands of times, and, much to his amusement, two cover versions of his famous song "Hallelujah" were top ten hits in 2008 after contestant Jason Castro performed the song on the hit television series *American Idol*.

SCENT

In part, I simply want to pause here and take stock of the deeper meaning of this popular and enduring singer-songwriter. Why do so many people around the world feel drawn to this artist, find they are caught up in his struggle and delight, and sing their lives by his lyrics and melodies? I've compared him to a flower—an especially haunting one, the gardenia, whose powerful scent seems achingly present even in its absence. Obviously, I do not intend to "explain" the genius of Leonard Cohen here. Such explanations are usually much less profound than the work they pretend to

make accessible. Rather, I am proposing to turn to some enduring themes as they surface in an intertwined set of works at the
center of Cohen's life and career: the 1984 album *Various Positions*
and the volume of poetry *Book of Mercy*, published in the same
year. These two works are, together, key aspects of the depth of
imagination and beauty in Cohen's art. Looking closely at four
themes in these works–tradition, calling, desire, and brokenness–
points us to the mysterious and compelling scent at the heart of
the flower.

The 1970s ended with the previously noted disastrous album
with Phil Spector, *Death of a Ladies' Man*, and the likewise disastrous ending to his longtime partnership with Suzanne Elrod,
who moved out, taking their children with her to Paris. A knee
injury at Mount Baldy prevented Cohen from meditating, and so
as he traveled between his home in Los Angeles, Montreal, and
Europe, he began to reengage his Jewish roots, seeking deeper
understanding of the mystical and spiritual roots of his own faith.
His depression, a continuing problem, had him by the throat, and
his experimental use of drugs to help his condition had long ago
become futile. He describes his state of mind at the time thus: "I
was silenced in all areas. I couldn't move." The only thing that
helped was the courage to "write down my prayers. To apply to the
source of mercy."[21] As he was nearing the age of fifty, he decided
to write a prayer for each year of his life. The numbered prayers
were published as *Book of Mercy*.

Writing the book was a highly personal task, and a healing
one as well: "The writing of it, in some ways, was the answer to
the prayer." *Book of Mercy* was also a work that gives way to the
practice of prayer. The cries that emerge from prayer after prayer
form an intense body of work. "You don't speak in that way,"
Cohen wrote of *Book of Mercy*, "unless you feel truly desperate
and you feel urgency in your life."[22] He felt anxious publishing the
book and was unsure of its genre; "it's not a quarrel, it's not an
argument, it's not theology; it is just asking."[23] The critics found
the spiritual subject matter of the book surprising, given that his
last book (and related album) were about the decidedly carnal topic
of the death of a ladies' man. Yet the power of *Book of Mercy*
was undeniable, and it won the Canadian Authors Association
Literature Prize for lyrical poetry.

Various Positions, released the same year, resulted from the same creative and spiritual mood. Cohen found songwriting increasingly difficult, and he needed the depth of spiritual searching to sustain his daily routine of writing. At one point, in the midst of working out the lyric for the fifth track, "Hallelujah," Cohen recalls being in his

> underwear crawling along the carpet in a shabby room at the Royalton Hotel unable to nail a verse. And knowing that I had a recording session and knowing that I could get by with what I had but that I'm not going to be able to do it.[24]

He realized that the initial wave of his popularity as a folksinger was over, that he was no longer–if he ever was–the voice of a generation. Digging down to his spiritual roots gave him new meaning, a kind of freedom from the ego's expectation.

Various Positions contains some of Cohen's best-known songs– and those he considers his best. Yet at the time, his record label, Columbia, was not at all sure that he was commercially viable. Walter Yetnikoff, president of the label, called Cohen into his New York office and said, "Look, Leonard; we know you're great, but we just don't know if you are any good."[25] Consequently, the record was released in Europe, where it was a modest success, but not in the United States. Cohen wryly called the CBS Building in New York, the home of Columbia, "the Tomb of the Unknown Record."[26] However, as the album grew in renown, it received a proper release six years later. Many concurred with Bob Dylan, who said at the time that Cohen's songs were becoming more like prayers. Indeed, and yet they only embody more clearly and deeply some of the core themes present throughout all of Cohen's life work. We'll work through four now, as a way to engage more closely with the product of his nights crawling on the floor, agonizing over words.

Tradition

Leonard Cohen defends his agonizing over words with recourse to biblical and ritual justification. In an interview from 1984, Robert Sward asked Cohen if he had found prayer as his natural language in *Book of Mercy* and *Various Positions*. Cohen responded,

I was touched as a child by the music and the kind of charged speech that I heard in the synagogue, where everything was important. . . . I always feel that the world was created through words, through speech in our tradition, and I've always seen the enormous light in charged speech, and that's what I've tried to get to. . . . That is where I squarely stand.[27]

An essential word in Cohen's tradition is the Name, "G-d," traditionally not written lest an unknowing person desecrate it (a tradition rooted in Deuteronomy 12). The Name has an inherent power, a holiness that comes from the very presence of God as creator and judge. In *Book of Mercy* poem 15, Cohen writes that when we call upon the Name, we are as beggars, before the Holy One. "How beautiful our heritage," he writes, "to have this way of speaking to eternity, how bountiful this solitude, surrounded, filled, and mastered by the Name, from which all things arise in splendor, depending one upon the other."[28]

Yet a key aspect of acknowledging the power of the Name and standing before such mercy is the ever-present reality of the law and human sinfulness. When an interviewer asked Cohen what occupation he would list on an application, he responded "Sinner."[29] In *Book of Mercy* he writes of again coming to God, "soiled by strategies and trapped in the loneliness" of his cramped space. He begs God to establish his "law in this walled place."[30] On *Various Positions'* third cut, titled "The Law," Cohen prays to God, who has called him many times, yet each time he has held back; each time he has been late. Later in the song, he confesses he can't claim the title of the "guilty" because "Guilty's too grand." From there, he moves into the chorus, reminding himself as much as anyone listening that "there's a Law." The truth of reality, for Cohen, is that the Torah offers a way of life rooted in justice and accountability, a form of life that includes a call to righteousness and the expectation of a "mighty Judgment coming," as he puts it in "Tower of Song."

The law also promises mercy and rest, a claim Cohen connects to the offer of Sabbath rest on the seventh day of creation (Gen. 2:2–4). In *Book of Mercy* a prayer begins, " 'Let me rest,' he cried from the panic at the top of his heap of days. 'Let me rest on the day of rest.' "[31] The day of rest is, of course, the Sabbath, a weekly spiritual practice Cohen has kept throughout his life. In a 2005 interview he noted,

> It's nice to have any peaceful moment, a moment that there is a form where you can relax in, and you don't have to improvise in, because usually when you live a life without a ritual form, you will have to continue to improvise, and I'm not so good at it. . . . So I'm very grateful when the kids and my friends come the Friday night, and I know what the form is, what the form of the meal is going to be, and what the tone is going to be, so for that reason it's very relaxing.[32]

Concluding the fifth prayer in *Book of Mercy*, Cohen describes the Torah singing to him, touching his hair, and giving him the gift of a crown that lifts the weight of his days till he can sing of how precious is this heritage, asking that the Lord lead him into the Sabbath. Here, then, the tradition becomes its own retreat, a kind of home for the exile, the stranger.

Calling

Another key aspect of Cohen's art as it intersects with spirituality is his self-understanding of being chosen for this work. It is, in the end, not his own voice, no matter the difficulty of his labors over the words. In the closing song on *Various Positions*, one of his most profound and haunting songs, "If It Be Your Will," Cohen lays down his own voice at the feet of the Voice upon whom he waits. "If it be your will," Cohen prays, "that I speak no more / and my voice be still / as it was before / I will speak no more," abiding until he is spoken for. This beautiful song, according to Cohen's biographer Ira Nadel, was borrowed from the Kol Nidre service closing Yom Kippur.[33] Just before a recounting of one's sins, the cantor cries out, "May it therefore be Your will, Lord our God, and God of our Fathers, to forgive us all our sins, to pardon all our iniquities, to grant us atonement for all our transgressions." The slow, somber melody is also derived from the ancient form of synagogue song for this service.

Cohen's voice is always working to be open to the Voice, the one who speaks through him and calls him out of silence into speech. In *Book of Mercy*'s prayer 10 he gives thanks that God has "sweetened" the word upon his lips. He goes on: "You placed me in this mystery and you let me sing," although just from this "curious corner." His humility is not false; it reflects his understanding of humanity in relation to God. Cohen describes his will as a "little will," working in its "curious corner." To really do his work, though, a kind of surrender must take place in which his "tiny will is annihilated, and thrown back into a kind of silence until you can make contact with another authentic thrust of your being. And we call that prayer when we can affirm it." He continues, "I think that in writing, when you're cooking as a writer, it is a destruction of the little will–you are operating on some other fuel."[34]

He reaches for the song, the poem, and yet knows the words come from elsewhere. *Book of Mercy*'s prayer 26 describes the challenge of sitting still in a chair while the dancer emerges from your very body: shoulders from shoulders, chest from chest, loins from loins, and "from your silence the throat makes a sound" so that through you God may "serve God in beauty." With regard to his vocation, Cohen exhibits a profound humility, founded in gratitude at times and exasperation at others. As I noted above, Cohen asks in *Book of Longing* (2006) why the Lord of his life has leaned him against the table in the middle of the night trying to write something beautiful. Yet in the end, Cohen confesses with a faithful awe, "You let me sing, you lifted me up."[35] He cries out in hopeful expectation that God would not let the words remain his own but that God would "change them into truth."[36]

Desire

Desire, the third theme at the center of Cohen's work, infuses all his work with a restlessness and energy. A commentator early in Cohen's career suggested that all his songs were about piety and sex. Indeed, Cohen himself has said only two things interest him: women and God. Yet his assertion was that to separate these two would be detrimental to both. If God is left out of sex, it becomes pornographic; if sex is left out of God, spirituality becomes self-righteous and pious.[37] For a silly example of God being left out of sex, one could turn to Cohen's 1970s song, "Don't Go Home With Your Hard-On," from *Death of a Ladies' Man*. On the whole, however, Cohen has been able to connect complicated desires in powerful and provocative ways. While fully admitting his "great appetite for the company of women," he also admits a continuing drive to escape to the "other side" of his life, a place of "solitude and quiet."[38] In prayer 20 of *Book of Mercy* Cohen evokes the image of an unborn child swimming toward birth and the woman in labor counting breaths as a way to speak of how he yearns for God. No matter the object, for Cohen there is an insistence, a desperation in his desire.

On *Various Positions*, "Coming Back to You" beautifully portrays the complex feelings of longing and desire. He claims he is still hurting from a lover's departure and can't yet "turn the other cheek." He searches for this lost love in others, but they know it and reject his misplaced desire. So he struggles with the paradox: while he admits to living alone, he nonetheless can see his future only as "coming back to you." With its slightly country-western swing, the song bears a certain sadness as he works his way through his feeling of being caught between his hurting, desiring love and the brokenness that prevents the reunion. The connection between brokenness and desire works to drive him to prayer. In *Book of Mercy* prayer 45, he confesses having lost his way, yet even there he makes his way to God. While he has wasted his days, he nonetheless says: "I bring the heap to you."

Yet the desire is sometimes broader than love of a person or of God. The lead song on *Various Positions*, "Dance Me to the End of Love," begins with an arresting image of dancing in the midst of both beauty and a burning violin, dancing "through the panic 'til I'm gathered safely in." With the female backup singers following a beat with their "la, la" and a slightly haunting violin entering later to pick up the tune from the piano, Cohen seems to be asking longingly for attention, for company, for a promise of hope against hope. In fact, the song intertwines a specific horror and hope against hope.

> "Dance me to the End of Love" . . . it's curious how songs begin because the origin of the song, every song, has a kind of grain or seed that somebody hands you or the world hands you and that's why the process is so mysterious about writing a song. But that came from just hearing or reading or knowing that in the death

camps, beside the crematoria, in certain of the death camps, a string quartet was pressed into performance while this horror was going on, those were the people whose fate was this horror also.[39]

Yet the song tenderly, insistently, powerfully articulates the longing for passion that transcends the brokenness. He calls for God to make a place of shelter now, even "though every thread is torn," as if this promise of love is behind, below, beyond all life's brokenness.

Brokenness

We've already begun to feel the weight of the final central theme I'd like to highlight in Cohen's work—brokenness. Cohen understands brokenness as evident in the world, and his understanding is attuned to suffering of many sorts. Early in his career, Cohen commented that in our age of convulsion and agony, we must

> rediscover the crucifixion. The crucifixion will again be understood as a universal symbol, not just an experiment in sadism or masochism or arrogance. It will have to be rediscovered because that's where [humanity] is at.[40]

While often described as a merely pessimistic writer, Cohen often follows the ancient psalms in offering both lament and promise in his descriptions of brokenness, as in "Dance me to the End of Love." *Book of Mercy*'s prayer 12 is perhaps the bleakest in the collection. A resentful voice jaded by the horrors of the world confesses pacing like an animal in "the corridor between my teeth and my bladder," harboring an "angry, murderous" feeling, and finding comfort only in "the smell of my sweat." Calling throughout for God to join us in the midst of our self-inflicted horrors, he concludes that in the brokenness of his own soul, he has fallen on both sides of a wedge he himself has driven into God's world. He begs for God to count him "back into [God's] mercy with the measures of a bitter song" and to allow him his tears as a way to pray out bodily, if you will, the bitterness of his circumstance.

His song emerges from this brokenness, a fact enlightenment or religion cannot finally save us from. He had hoped, at one point, that Buddhism could help him escape. His hard-earned wisdom, however, is this:

> The religious promise is very cruel–that if you get enlightened you can live without suffering. And that's very cruel, because no one can live without suffering, there are just too many things that happen in life to ever present that guarantee, regardless of how rigorous the religious discipline is. It doesn't matter how advanced or fulfilled or enlightened an individual is, it will never be free of the sorrows and the pains of the moment. If someone steps on his toe he is going to cry out, and if someone steps on his heart he is going to cry out.[41]

This mood is captured in the song "If It Be Your Will," from *Various Positions*. There, Cohen sings that if it be God's will that his voice sing out true, then "from this broken hill / I will sing to you." To be truly human, Cohen argues, brokenness becomes part of our prayer. "All my life is broken unto you," he prays in *Book of Mercy*'s prayer 49.

The sentiment of broken life offered up in prayer comes to a pinnacle in his much-loved song from *Various Positions*, "Hallelujah."[42] "Hallelujah" is the kind of song that seems as if it has always been written. Of course, that is partly because its main theme, the chorus "Hallelujah," has indeed always been written. It is the ancient Hebrew word "הַלְלוּיָהּ" (*Hallĕlûyâh*), meaning "praise God," and is found over and over in Psalms. The song has also resonated because of the interplay of the music and lyrics. The simple, subtle tune bears the words along, rising through the verses to a climax of a ringing chorus of voices singing hallelujah. The lyric has an obvious religious depth, drawing explicitly or implicitly on various biblical images. The song first references King David, well known both as a musical genius and as a womanizer, as well as Samson, the judge of Israel who was undone by telling Delilah that cutting his hair would strip him of his strength. The third verse connects the Name with the blaze of light in words given by the Creator, and also to the exodus, where Moses learns "the name" of G-d.

It is, however, not "just" a biblical song. It draws from those roots to speak about both the power of the holy and the brokenness of human life. While the song begins with David, it moves progressively out of the Bible and into the challenges of daily life. The last verse speaks to the challenge of living. A deep humility about human goodness comes through as Cohen sings that he's done all he could, though in the end "it wasn't much." Perhaps this is easier to say in Canada, but for the eternally optimistic "Your Best Life Now" America, such sentiment is dismissed as misguided–a downer at best and unfaithful at worst.[43] Theologically, however, I think Cohen is spot-on, getting exactly at what a faithful life means. In this life, all we are capable of is a broken hallelujah. And the fact that we're able to raise even a broken hallelujah results from what God has done for us. Cohen said,

> I wanted to write something in the tradition of the hallelujah choruses but from a different point of view. . . . It's the notion that there is no perfection–that this is a broken world and we live with broken hearts and broken lives but still that is no alibi for anything. On the contrary, you have to stand up and say hallelujah under those circumstances.[44]

Knowing that keeps us from trying to please God with our shiny "holy hallelujahs" and allows us to be honest about ourselves, our need for God's mercy, and our call to join in God's mission of mercy in the midst of a broken world.

Why does Leonard Cohen's music have this fragrance about it? A powerful haunting attractiveness not unlike, as I've suggested playfully above, the beautiful gardenia flower Cohen often had on his writing desk during his years on Hydra. Tradition, calling, desire, and brokenness. These themes are evident throughout his life–especially in his key mid-1980s work in *Book of Mercy* and *Various Positions*–and go some way to making sense. One further element needs to be set clearly before us, and to do so provides a hint about the question driving the next chapter: why does God love the blues? This further element has already been present implicitly–the need to speak of the brokenness of the world and sing it to God requires unflinching honesty. Asked by an interviewer why his music is so relentlessly stark and revealing, Cohen responded:

It was all I could write about. . . . You have to dig down for that true voice, which you've heard in others–a Billie Holiday or a Hank Williams–and you try to find it in your music. It's a way of proving you deserve to be here. . . . You deserve to get a girl or deserve to walk out on the street. I know this is a very poverty-stricken view of things, but that's the way it was. I never had the luxury of standing in front of a buffet table saying, "I'll write this kind of song today and that kind tomorrow." It was like: "Can I scrape some words together and write anything? . . . Can I dig deep enough inside to say something that matters?"[45]

3

WHY GOD LOVES THE BLUES

Why are you so down in the dumps, dear soul?
Why are you crying the blues?

—Psalm 43:5

STRANGE FRUIT

Late one evening in 1939 the patrons at a Manhattan nightclub knew something unusual was about to happen. Café Society, an unusually progressive club that welcomed white and black as both performers and audience members, had a full house that night. The twenty-four-year-old featured artist had already gained a reputation as a unique and moving interpreter of popular songs such as "What a Little Moonlight Can Do."[1] But this night, before the final song of Billie Holiday's set, the servers stopped serving, cigarettes were snuffed out, and the house lights were turned down, save a single spotlight. The light illumined only her face, as if she were standing under a dim streetlight. The song began with Frankie Newton's muted trumpet crying out in repeated descending lines, giving way to Sonny White's hushed, mournful piano. Leaning into the microphone, half-standing, half-sitting on a stool, Holiday slowly began her now-classic lament recalling the trees of the South bearing "strange fruit," black bodies bloodied and swinging in the breeze. Not a glass clinked; not a muffled cough could be heard in the club. With an artfully restrained tempo and emotion, she continued singing, the lyrics dripping with irony. The juxtaposition of classic images of the South such as sweet magnolia blossoms alongside the arresting image of burning flesh builds to a final line impossible to hear without being gripped in emotion: "Here is a strange and bitter crop." She brought the song to a beautiful, horrifying end by holding a high note on "crop" as if seeing the hanging bodies in her mind's eye. Then the light cut out, and she walked off the stage. After a period of stunned silence, one lone person nervously began to clap, then the whole audience joined. Many in the audience openly wept and word about the daring song quickly spread.[2]

There are many versions of the story of how Billie Holiday came to sing "Strange Fruit," and each tends to make its teller seem especially relevant to the story. Unsurprisingly, the white men who served as her managers and handlers make themselves out to be the wise ones, and Billie to be oblivious and obedient, something she contests in her autobiography.

Despite conflicting stories, some facts seem clear: Abel Meeropol, a New York City schoolteacher, wrote the song under his pen name Lewis Allan. An avid poet and songwriter allied with progressive causes of the time, Meeropol supposedly saw a photograph of the infamous August 7, 1930, lynching of Tom Shipp and Abe Smith in Marion, Indiana. The two men were captured and charged with robbery, murder, and rape. An angry mob broke into the Grant County jail, brutally beat the men to death, and hung them from a tree in the town square. Local photographer Lawrence Beitler captured a surreal scene that portrays some of the thousands who gathered for the spectacle: men in ties and banded straw hats, women in dresses, with one man in the center pointing upward toward the bloodied bodies hanging limply from ropes thrown over branches in the tree.[3] Deeply moved by the photograph, Meeropol penned the poem and developed a melody for the song that he and a few others sang at school meetings and union gatherings.

While much of America was mobbing theaters to see *Gone with the Wind*, Meeropol asked–or was invited, depending on which story you choose–to share the song with Holiday. Barney Josephson, manager of Café Society, negotiated the meeting. Again accounts vary, but it is clear that despite others wanting credit for her decision to sing the song, it was Holiday herself who felt called to add it to her repertoire despite real risks of retaliation. She recalled:

> It was during my stint at Café Society that a song was born which became my personal protest–"Strange Fruit." The germ of the song was in a poem written by Lewis Allan. I first met him at Café Society. When he showed me that poem, I dug it right off. It seemed to spell out all the things that had killed Pop.[4]

Her father, jazz guitarist Clarence Holiday, died just two years prior to her singing "Strange Fruit." Suffering from exposure to mustard gas while serving in World War I had weakened his lungs. When he caught a cold on tour with Don Redman's band in Texas, Pop knew he needed special care. Rather than risk refusal or second-class care at hospitals in rural Texas, he planned to wait until the band reached Dallas's Veterans Hospital. But by the time the band reached Dallas, pneumonia had set in and he died shortly after.[5]

As with her father, Billie Holiday's many experiences of racial discrimination offered ample opportunity to resonate with the emotional edge of "Strange Fruit." Recalling her first (and only) opportunity at the big screen, opposite Louis Armstrong in the film *New Orleans* (1947), Holiday reveals her anger at discovering she would "star" in the role of a maid:

> I thought I was going to play myself in it. I thought I was going to be Billie Holiday doing a couple of songs in a nightclub setting and that would be that. I should have known better. When I saw the script, I did. You just tell me one Negro girl who's made movies who didn't play a maid or a whore. I don't know any. I found out I was going to do a little singing, but I was still playing the part of a maid.[6]

She made "Strange Fruit" her signature song, even changing her contract to stipulate her right to perform it. She did this to counteract club owners who regularly sought to bar its performance. Her own mother, Sadie Fagan, worried about her safety and asked, "Why are you sticking your neck out?" Holiday replied, "Because it might make things better."[7]

Billie Holiday knew that the song might not make her career better, no matter what long-term changes she might have hoped for in society. John Hammond, the talent scout who brokered her first recording contract on the Columbia label, said that singing the song was "the worst [artistic] thing that ever happened to Billie."[8] But drummer Max Roach had a different opinion, an opinion shared by many: "When [Billie] recorded ["Strange Fruit"], it was more than revolutionary. She made a statement that we all felt as black folks."[9] Abel Meeropol said, "Billie Holiday's styling of the song was incomparable and fulfilled the bitterness and shocking quality I had hoped the song would have [when I wrote it]. The audience gave her a tremendous ovation."[10] Samuel Grafton, a *New York Post* columnist, was deeply moved by the power of the song and wrote: "The polite conversations between race and race are gone. It is as if we heard what was spoken in the cabins, after the night riders had clattered by."[11]

Indeed, the prominence of the song did lend energy to the decades-long battle by NAACP leaders and others to sponsor and institute a national antilynching law. Unfortunately, bills were introduced and passed three times in the House of Representatives only to be stopped by filibusters in the Senate. It is a significant piece of the horror of lynching in the US that as a result of this Senate inaction a national antilynching law was never passed. The Senate publicly apologized for this failure in 2005.[12]

Most of Billie Holiday's songs were not about political protest, at least not directly. They were songs about love and loss, typical fare for popular music and for the blues in particular. In fact, "Strange Fruit" was released on a 78 rpm record with Holiday's own composition "Fine and Mellow" as the B side. Written the night before the recording session, "Fine and Mellow" ruminates on the plight of a woman being treated poorly by her man. While only twenty-four when she wrote and recorded this song, Holiday had seen enough of life to sing powerfully from the experience of suffering.

Eleanora Fagan (Holiday's birth name) was born in Philadelphia in 1915 to Sadie Fagan. Her father, Clarence Holiday, was a traveling jazz guitarist who left before she was born and apparently didn't acknowledge his paternity until she became famous many years later. Raised by her mother in very difficult circumstances in Philadelphia and New York, Holiday recalls being raped multiple times before she was fifteen. During her teens she worked as a prostitute, eventually spending a year in prison for solicitation. She had begun singing earlier, in nightclubs and brothels, but after prison she finally got a break singing for tips in Harlem nightclubs, where Columbia Records talent scout John Hammond heard her. By age eighteen she had cut her first record, chosen for her by John Hammond and recorded with Benny Goodman.

As Holiday began to write her own songs, such as "Fine and Mellow," she drew powerfully on the blues mode. Jazz great Wynton Marsalis observed:

> When you hear Billie Holiday sing, you hear the spirit of Bessie Smith and Louis Armstrong together in a person, so you have the fire of the blues shouter, you have the intelligent choice of notes like a great jazz musician, but with her you have a profound sensitivity to the human condition. She tells you something about the pain of the blues, of life, but inside of that pain is a toughness and that's what you are attracted to.[13]

"Fine and Mellow" became one of her characteristic tunes. Many versions of the song exist, but perhaps her best live recording took place in December 1957 on the live telecast of a CBS program called *The Sound of Jazz*.[14] For the recording she reconnected with her old friend, saxophone great Lester Young. Just before she begins to sing, one hears an overdub of Holiday's voice commenting about the blues: "The blues to me is like being very sad, being sick . . . the blues is sort of a mixed-up thing. You just have to feel it. Anything I do sing is part of my life." Dressed simply in pants, white shirt, and cardigan, Holiday takes her characteristic stance amid the instrumentalists, half-standing, half-sitting on a stool. As the saxophones slowly swing into the sad tune marked by classic blues descending thirds, Holiday gently unfolds the first verse in AAB form about her "man" who "don't love me" and "treats me oh so mean." He is, she persuades us, "the lowest man, that I've ever seen." Saxophone solos follow, including an incredibly moving and subtle solo by Lester Young, with an impassioned Holiday clearly urging him on.

If she was mainly known for lighthearted love songs like "It Was Just One of Those Things," the blues as represented in "Fine and Mellow" were closer to Billie Holiday's life experience.[15] She suffered a series of abusive relationships with men, usually interwoven with her abuse of drugs and alcohol—a contributing factor to her death at the young age of forty-four. Yet her legacy has only grown since her death, a legacy rooted in her brilliant innovations as a vocalist and her willingness to raise race questions.

Holiday remarked on more than one occasion, "I'm a race woman." Of touring, she lamented, "I hardly ever ate, slept, or went to the bathroom without having a major NAACP-type production," a reality of the still-strong segregation policies in many regions where she traveled and played.[16] Even in more progressive urban areas, white audiences could be impervious to her message, as when a woman at a Los Angeles club asked Holiday to sing "that sexy song you're so famous for, you know, the one about the naked bodies swinging in the trees."[17] If one understands something of the profound pain of her life with stories such as these, then one can understand her determination to take a stand, concert after concert, singing what may be the most moving, if horrible, love song of her career—a love song for her people, rooted in the prophet's cry against injustice.

DEVIL'S MUSIC

It is ironic, given the social and political complaint in Billie Holiday's evocation of the blues tradition, that so much commentary, scholarly and popular, describes the blues as "the devil's music." Wouldn't such lament, either about abusive relationships on a personal level or sociopolitical issues, be worthy of careful attention by people of faith? That label "the devil's music," however, constitutes one reason many people of faith might hold such music at arm's length. And so, before going further, we must explore this characterization. In trying to get behind the satanic representation of this music, we'll be able to see both the truth and the limits of such claims. In the end, I will argue that the blues are "secular spirituals" that arise from the same root as the powerful laments Scripture itself teaches us to lift before God.

The understanding of the blues as the devil's music does go back to the early twentieth century, when these haunting songs were first played on the porches and in the juke joints and barrelhouses of the Mississippi Delta. The music was associated with drinking, gambling, dancing, and illicit sex, things shunned by churchgoing folk and condemned by their preachers. Such a fact is one obvious reason for its categorization as sinners' music. There are also many stories of musicians–Robert Johnson being the most famous–selling their souls to the devil in exchange for great musical talent.

However, the music as a whole, and its mythology of the devil, remained limited primarily to African American communities in the South and in northern cities such as Chicago and New York. This was partly because much of the early or "country" blues music was released on so-called race labels created in the 1920s for distribution to the newly discovered African American market. But social factors, including the urbanization and the upheaval of the Great Depression, Great Migration, and World War II years, shifted the record industry away from the "country" blues.

A major turn of fortune for both the blues and the interpretation of them as the devil's music came as a result of the British blues revival in the late 1950s and early 1960s. Three interconnected forces of this era influenced why the blues are widely viewed as "the devil's music" today. The first and perhaps most obvious force resulted from R&B stars like Bo Diddley. Diddley depended on and popularized the blues of John Lee Hooker, Muddy Waters, and others who had brought the old country blues tradition to the city, transforming the tradition by using electric guitars and more urban themes.

In the mid-1950s Muddy Waters, Sonny Boy Williamson, Howlin' Wolf, and other "rediscovered" bluesmen toured the UK. These tours, and their subsequent effect on the development of British rock and roll, were the second significant force that shaped our current understanding of the blues. The Metropolitan Blues Quartet–later known as the Yardbirds–was formed in London in 1962 and included three men who would become the most influential guitarists of early rock and roll: Eric Clapton, Jimmy Page, and Jeff Beck. Among them, Eric Clapton is perhaps most important.

He later formed the band Cream and has single-handedly lifted Robert Johnson's profile through his career-long tributes. He performed a classic cover of Johnson's "Crossroads" with Cream in the early 1970s and recorded a tribute album in 2004 titled *Me and Mr. Johnson.*

Page went on to found Led Zeppelin, the quintessential rock-and-roll band of the 1970s. Page's embrace of the blues contributed much to Zeppelin's sound and success (although Zeppelin's debt to the blues was mostly unacknowledged–Chess Records, a Chicago blues label, and individual artists sued the band for songwriting credit and royalties).[18] Emerging from the same early 1960s London blues clubs, the Rolling Stones took their name from a Muddy Waters song and in 1962 set out to be the best blues band in England.

The aging bluesmen–Muddy Waters, Sonny Boy Williamson, Howlin' Wolf–found it both compelling and humorous to see young white people so crazy over their music while these bluesmen were losing ground in the US to the new sounds of Bo Diddley and Elvis Presley. Sonny Boy Williamson even toured Europe with the Yardbirds as his backup band, famously saying of the experience, "Those English kids want to play the blues so bad–and they play the blues *so* bad!"[19]

What was it that these British youth wanted so badly to obtain? In an interview on NPR, Eric Clapton recalls first hearing Robert Johnson's blues as a teenager:

> I was definitely overwhelmed, but I was also a bit repelled by the intensity of it. . . . I kind of got hooked on it because it was so much more powerful than anything else I had heard or was listening to. Amongst all of his peers I felt he was the one that was talking from his soul without really compromising for anybody.[20]

In an interview on *Larry King Live*, Clapton got deeper into the nature of his attraction and inadvertently raised some of the problems with the British revival of the blues, and white appropriation of the blues more generally. "You know what it was," Clapton told Larry King, "it was primitive. I think it was primitive, and it sounded like it was unattached to any kind of corporative thinking, you know what I mean? It was like a guy, one guy who was on his own real in a kind of madness."[21] It is condescending enough to describe Johnson's brilliant music as "primitive" or arising from "madness," but it unfortunately opens the door to idealizing myths about the blues originating in a pact with the devil.

The third force shaping contemporary understandings of the blues as "devil's music" resulted from the historical studies of the origins of the blues by British blues enthusiasts. These first book-length investigations offered a perspective that, while not wholly wrong, bore within them serious misinterpretation of the roots of the blues. For instance, Paul Oliver, an English architectural historian, encouraged the revival of interest in the blues through his groundbreaking books, including *Blues Fell This Morning*, released in 1960.

While Oliver's work went a long way toward interpreting the social and historical context of the blues within African American social life, because he was an outsider to that culture his work had inevitable limits. Writing more than thirty years later, theologian and ethnomusicologist Jon Michael Spencer suggested that the most important limit for outsiders to the culture that produced the blues is the failure to "capture the music's pervading ethos—its religious nature!"[22] For example, Spencer cites Oliver's position that "for the most part the blues is strictly secular in content. The old-time religion of the southern churches did not permit the singing of 'devil songs' and 'jumped-up' songs as the blues were commonly termed."[23] Such a framing, Spencer argues, shows how Oliver imposes "Christianity's bifurcating worldview (the sacred versus the profane) on the holistic cosmology of this people of African origin."[24]

Oliver's work paved the way for Giles Oakley's five-part BBC documentary and companion book, titled *The Devil's Music: A History of the Blues*. This work, feeding off the powerful ethos of rock and roll increasingly tied to experimentation with drugs and "free love," fed the fire of a growing fascination with devil lore in blues music. Oakley responsibly noted that the label "the devil's music" was given "by (usually black) opponents who have feared its power as a social force, whether for 'disruption,' 'irresponsibility,' 'irreligion,' or for sexual freedom."[25] Without careful attention to culture and context, fans and followers of the blues simply embraced the myth of sex and the devil as an element of the countercultural music.

Such mythology centered on Robert Johnson, who famously traded his soul to the devil at the crossroads to gain his musical (and likely also sexual) prowess.[26] Popular writing about Johnson often resorts to colorful stereotypes: that Johnson was, for instance, "the original singer of American evil who played like the devil and died like a dog," supposedly barking on all fours as the devil demanded his soul in payment.[27]

Spencer argues that since Johnson was likely poisoned with strychnine-laced whiskey by a jealous husband of one of his many lovers, he quite possibly seemed delirious, fell on the floor, and even perhaps "barfed," which, as the story evolved over time, turned into "barking" like a dog.[28] Such events unfortunately are bent to fit the fantasies of white fans drawn to the devil mythology suggested in his music.

Extensive interviews and field research have produced a much more nuanced portrayal of Robert Johnson's life, including ideas rooted in the West African culture brought by the slaves, especially that of Legba, a trickster god often found at crossroads. Legba was known as a god of good and evil, sacred and profane, male and female.[29] Such a trickster personage allowed Johnson–as it did other musicians–to claim the devil as their relation (father, uncle) to gain attention and notoriety, building the crowds as they traveled and played. The multiple valences–both African and European Protestant–of their language allowed talk of the devil to carry multiple nuances that were lost in translation to white urban youth of the 1950s and 1960s. Spencer notes that as a result, the blues gradually lost its original religiousness born in the complex culture of the Delta.[30]

One can see this transition even in the lifetime of a blues singer who made the transition from country to urban blues: Muddy Waters. While his early songs echoed both African religious traces ("Got My Mojo Working," "mojo" being a traditional form of West African magic) and Protestant Christian forms ("I Can't Be Satisfied," with its intermittent cry, "Lord"), Waters's last studio session in 1981 offered the song "Champagne and Reefer," an homage to his favorite mood-changing substances. For Muddy Waters, as for much of the blues tradition, the story is not as simple as music on the side of God or the devil, despite the tendency of many blues fans to have, as the Rolling Stones later referenced, "sympathy for the devil."[31] Yet the relationship between the juke joint and its pulsing blues and the clapboard church with its swelling organ gospels is a key to getting at the truth of our story. To that relationship we now turn.

SATURDAY NIGHT–SUNDAY MORNING

Most white scholars, Spencer notes, misconstrue the "so-called 'atheism' of the blues as nothing more than a polemical moment for blues singers to stand in opposition to a history of oppression by white 'theists' (Christians), a polemical moment that by no means precluded blues being fundamentally religious."[32]

However, the truth is that a version of Protestant Christianity that separates good and evil, soul and body, church hymns and the blues deeply marked the culture of African Americans in the South generally and the blues players in particular. Alan Lomax, the extraordinary folk music scholar whose field recordings helped popularize many early blues players, recalled this encounter on the Smithers Plantation near Huntsville, Texas, in the 1930s. After Lomax explained what he was looking for, the manager brought in a man by the name of "One-Eye Charley." Lomax writes:

> The manager said: "One-Eye, these gentlemen want to hear some real, old-time nigger singin', not hymns, but some of the songs you've sort of made up out in the field, choppin' cotton or plowin' with the mules."
>
> By this time One-Eye had strained his head up and away from us until it was impossible to catch his eye. Through his patched and tattered shirt, one could see the sweat bursting out and streaming down his hairy chest.
>
> "I ain't no kind of a songster myself, boss. 'Cose I do hum dese here sancrified hymns sometimes, but I'se a member of de chu'ch an' I done clean forgot all de wor'ly songs I ever knowed."[33]

The question of what it might mean that One-Eye, faced with a white man who wanted to record his songs, claimed to have "done clean forgot all de wor'ly songs I ever knowed" divides scholarship on the blues.

One perspective is to read the divide as strict separation. Paul Oliver argued that the relation of blues to the gospel–of Saturday night to Sunday morning–is literally like night and day. The blues is a secular form cast out from the church: "Blues that is performing a specifically religious function may scarcely be said to exist."[34] For a case in point, he turned to "Foolin' Blues" by Texas bluesman J. T. "Funny Paper" Smith. In the song, Smith sings about God taking care of "old folks and fools" but then complains that "since I've been born he must have changed the rules." Smith asks God questions, wondering aloud "was there any mercy left." In the third verse he claims he is asking God "every day" to forgive his sins. He worries that rather than Jesus, "it must be the devil I'm servin,' " because after asking him for salvation, he "tried to take my life."[35]

Oliver responded to this lyric by claiming that "blues is somewhat bereft of spiritual values." "Lower-class Blacks often had to decide whether to accept with meekness the cross they had to bear in this world and to join the church with the promise of 'Eternal Peace in the Promised Land' or whether to attempt to meet the present world on its own terms, come what may." Oliver concludes, "The blues singer chose the latter course."[36]

Part of the problem here is Oliver's misinterpretation of the culture and context of African American life. Angela Davis takes appropriate offense at Oliver's portrayal of southern black people "primarily concerned with the business of living day-to-day, of 'getting along' with the Whites, of conforming and making the best of their circumstances."[37] There is no excuse, Davis retorted, for representing blacks as mere victims of circumstances. Blacks did indeed survive by what W. E. B. Du Bois called a "two-ness" or a "double-consciousness," one used in relation to the master to survive and another when out of earshot of whites.[38] But to collapse the complexity of the double-consciousness into mere acquiescence is to miss how the foil of "getting by" made space for all manner of resistance tactics, even in the time of slavery and the disappointment of the post–Civil War Reconstruction era, out of which the blues arose.

Oliver wrote in the late 1950s, as Davis notes: "Such a position is especially offensive considering the fact that the era during which [Oliver] wrote this book–the years following the Montgomery bus boycott–was the beginning of one of the most influential social movements in modern world history."[39]

Misunderstanding the overall cultural context directly relates to Oliver's portrayal of the stark divide between spirituals and the blues, between the sacred and the secular. Jon Michael Spencer argues that a more accurate understanding would be that the spirituals and the blues were part of one culture in dialogue within the blues singers themselves. Responding to "Foolin' Blues," quoted above, Spencer writes that speaking the truth, a virtue rooted in a shared moral universe between church and the blues, sometimes called for an ostensibly sacrilegious critique of God. Quoting bluesman Henry Townsend, Spencer makes his point:

> Some people think that the blues is something that is evil–I don't. . . . If the blues is delivered in the truth, which most of them are . . . if I sing the blues and tell the truth, what have I done? What have I committed? I haven't lied.[40]

Here, Spencer argues, we hear a version of the beatitudes–"Blessed are those who bear no false witness"–articulated by the blues over against the "hypocrisy and self-righteousness of the churched."[41]

In the moving last chapter to his famous work *The Souls of Black Folk*, W. E. B. Du Bois characterized the slave spirituals as "Sorrow Songs" in a way that shows their interconnection with the culture that produced the blues. They are, Du Bois wrote, "the music of an unhappy people, of the children of disappointment; they tell of death and suffering and unvoiced longing toward a truer world, of misty wanderings and hidden ways."

Yet, Du Bois noted, time and again throughout the Sorrow Songs, the "minor cadences of despair" turn to the "sound of Jubilee" in anticipation of the justice of God and another world beyond the reality of daily suffering. This haunted Du Bois, as he was sensitive to the fact that they had precious little evidence in the midst of their lives to justify such hope. He wondered what sustained this seemingly blind hope that "sometime, somewhere, men will judge men by their souls and not by their skins." Du Bois rhetorically asks: "Is such a hope justified? Do the Sorrow Songs sing true?"[42]

In the first serious treatment of the blues as religious music, theologian James Cone picks up on Du Bois's question of the spirituals singing true. Cone contends that when the blues and the spirituals are considered together, it is clear that "the blues and the spirituals flow from the same bedrock of experience, and neither is an adequate interpretation of black life without the commentary of the other."[43] Calling the blues "secular spirituals," Cone points out how the blues take as their subject the "secular" in the sense that they chronicle "the immediate and affirm the bodily expression of the black soul, including sexual manifestations." Yet they are "spirituals" insofar as "they are impelled by the same search for the truth of black experience."[44] The particular truth of experience leading to the blues, Cone argues, was the frustration a generation after emancipation in the face of the social and legal disenfranchisement of black people.

Still, despite constraints on every side, the basic freedoms of emancipation—allowing choice in love and marriage, as well as of movement from town to town—meant new gathering places emerged beyond the church. And from these new sites the blues preachers "proclaimed the Word of black existence, depicting its joy and sorrow, love and hate, and the awesome burden of being 'free' in a racist society when one is black." The center of this Word is their character of truth-telling. The blues, Cone argues, is synonymous with speaking the truth of life, the life of "being black in a white racist society."[45]

The complexity of the connection between the blues and the spirituals, between Saturday night and Sunday morning, between the pain of life and the struggle to sing truthfully about it, is embodied in the lives of blues singers themselves.[46] While many singers I've already mentioned—from Robert Johnson to Muddy Waters—might serve as blues examples, I'll next focus on a pair who worked together and exemplify the Saturday night–Sunday morning dialogue. Gertrude Pridgett Rainey, known as "Ma" Rainey, is known as the "mother of the blues" for her alleged role in naming these sorrowful songs "the blues." "Georgia Tom" Dorsey was Rainey's pianist and bandleader during the peak years of her career and went on to become known as the father of gospel.

Ma Rainey as a case study continues a recent effort by Angela Davis and others to correct overemphasis on male blues singers.[47] I also focus on Rainey's connection to Dorsey—rather than the typical story told of Rainey's influence on Bessie Smith. This move counters the deaf ear much blues scholarship has turned to religion, which, as I've said above, is a key thematic element shared by *both* the spirituals and the blues.[48]

Ma Rainey

Ma Rainey left her birthplace of Columbus, Georgia, at sixteen, after achieving some local renown at a local talent show called "Bunch of Blackberries." On the road with a popular vaudeville and minstrel show in the spring of 1902, she recalled one stop in Missouri:

> [Ma] tells of a girl from the town who came to the tent one morning and began to sing about the "man" who had left her. The song was so strange and poignant that it attracted much attention. "Ma" Rainey became so interested that she learned the song from the visitor, and used it soon afterward in her act as an encore. The song elicited such response from the audience that it won a special place in her act. Many times she was asked what kind of song it was, and one day she replied, in a moment of inspiration, "It's the *blues*."[49]

Rainey told this story to Fisk University musicologist John Wesley Work Jr. in the late 1930s. She said as she traveled she heard many more of these "strange songs" and incorporated them into her acts.
  In 1904, at age eighteen, she met and married William "Pa" Rainey, a traveling manager for the Rabbit's Foot Minstrel Show, one of the most popular at that time.[50] After only a few years, they separated and Ma traveled under her own name, enjoying large audiences attracted by her vocal and performance style, described as raw, moaning, and yet exquisite in phrasing and originality.[51] Her mastery of the blues–both traditional and her own originals–connected to an audience of mainly poor, rural sharecroppers. The blues, after all, emerged from the life "behind the mule," and its moans and cries were ones Rainey knew well.[52]

By the time she was invited to record with the small Wisconsin label Paramount Records, in 1923, Rainey had already established a widespread reputation as a blues singer and entertainer. Mamie Smith had recorded the first blues record just a few years earlier, but her northern sophistication didn't connect to the southern audience as well as Rainey's performing, with its rougher, down-home feeling. Rainey recorded again in 1924 (with backing from a young Louis Armstrong on such hits as "See See Blues" and "Countin' the Blues," discussed below). Her record sales led Paramount to book a tour of the Theater Owner's Booking Agency, a circuit of mostly black and interracial theaters in major southern and midwestern cities.[53]

In preparation for this tour, Rainey formed a band built around Dorsey, who had heard her play years before when he worked concessions at the 81 Theater in Atlanta. He had moved up to Chicago a few years earlier and was playing around the city. Billing himself as "Georgia Tom" and his band as the "Wildcats Jazz Band," Dorsey opened Rainey's tour with a successful concert at the Grand Theater. Dorsey recalls that Rainey was "grand, gracious and easy to talk to." He described her as a dramatic presence onstage. Starting with soft lights and the band playing, Ma Rainey began singing in a large box built like an old Victrola record player.

> Then she would open the door and step out into the spotlight with her glittering gown that weighed twenty pounds and wearing a necklace of five, ten and twenty dollar gold-pieces. The house went wild. . . . When Ma had sung her last number and the grand finale, we took seven [curtain] calls.[54]

Dorsey served as tour manager, songwriter, and bandleader, while his young wife, Nettie Harper, served as Rainey's wardrobe mistress. Unfortunately, the stress of the frenetic touring life caused Dorsey to have a nervous breakdown, and he returned to Chicago to recover.

Blues scholar Sandra Lieb writes that "the body of Ma Rainey's recorded songs constitutes a message to women, explaining quite clearly how to deal with reverses in love and how to interpret other areas of life." Despite the image of the blues as sorrow songs, Rainey's songs show "an astonishing range of emotional reactions to misfortune, from misery to rage and from humor to cynicism."[55]

Many of the songs show women taking initiative in addressing the challenges they face despite their feelings of misery. In "Misery Blues," an original composition, Rainey sings about being the fool who loves her man, gives him her money because he said he loved her and would marry her, and instead he leaves her alone and broke. Jilted and broke, she sings, "I've got the blues, the misery blues." Even as she sings the blues, however, she contemplates going "to work now, to get another start."[56]

While many songs represent women's ambiguous relationships with men, especially with issues of disrespect, unfaithfulness, and violence, one song makes obvious what was often rumored: Rainey's sexual relationships with women. In her bold "Prove It on Me Blues," Rainey sings that she went out but got into a fight, and when she looked up, "the gal I was with was gone." She sings that she had gone out "last night with a crowd of my friends / They must've been women, 'cause I don't like no men." In her defense, she simply challenges that although she's been accused, "ain't nobody caught me / sure got to prove it on me." She evokes the "butch" stereotype, singing, "It's true I wear a collar and tie" and "talk to the gals just like any old man."[57]

Only on one occasion was she caught. At a party with a few other ladies in Chicago, the noise level caused a neighbor to call the police, who arrived just as the party turned intimate. Ma, running out the back door clutching someone else's dress, fell down the stairs and was apprehended. It was Bessie Smith who bailed her out of jail the next morning.[58] Rainey's relationship with Smith–a younger and equally successful blues singer she met while touring her hometown of Chattanooga, Tennessee–was one of her most prominent. Thomas Dorsey, who worked at the 81 during those years, confirms that Ma took Bessie under her wing, coaching her in singing the blues.[59]

While much has been made of the song "Prove It on Me" and related stories, Angela Davis's incisive commentary seems exactly right: in writing and singing such songs, Rainey and others like her were "defining the blues as a site where women could articulate and communicate their protests against male dominance."[60]

Such meditation on the blues as a site for speaking the truth occasionally took an explicitly religious turn. "Countin' the Blues," a beautifully played, soulfully sung blues, features Louis Armstrong on cornet, Coleman Hawkins on tenor saxophone, and other members of Fletcher Henderson's band in New York. As banjo, clarinet, and trumpet ring out their first notes, one can hear Ma Rainey calling, "Lord, I got the blues this mornin', I want everyone to go down in prayer, Lord, Lord." She then recounts lying in her bed, face turned to the wall, trying to count all the blues she could name so she could sing them. The song counts fourteen blues songs in all, naming them one by one, calling on the Lord each time. By doing so, Davis argues that "Rainey consciously reconfigures the blues as prayer." Davis suggests Rainey is drawing upon a West African tradition of "nommo," which "conjures powers associated with things by ritually pronouncing their names."[61] Davis connects this as a parallel practice to the biblical witness of God's creative word, showing how this litany of blues names puts at the singer's disposal what she needs "to try to dream away my troubles, countin' those blues."[62]

Rainey kept touring and recording throughout the twenties, including a significant recording session in 1928 with Dorsey, now partnered with bottleneck-guitar player Hudson "Tampa Red" Whittaker, whose hit song "It's Tight Like That" was all the rage. Yet in just a few years, the Great Depression brought changing fortunes and tastes. Declining opportunity, combined with the deaths of Rainey's mother and sister, led to her retirement to Columbus, Georgia, in 1935. She had purchased two theaters in town, the Airdrome and the Lyric, perhaps anticipating the move. She lived her last years with her brother, Thomas Pridgett Jr., a deacon at Friendship Baptist Church, where Ma became a devoted member, singing and doing volunteer work.

While she was a huge success in the 1920s, her relatively circumscribed travel (mostly in the South) and the poor-quality recordings made by her label, Paramount, contributed to Ma Rainey's legacy languishing in relative obscurity. As scholars—and especially women—began to write about the blues, Ma Rainey's truly legendary role was rehabilitated. One beautiful moment in this revival is the outstanding American playwright August Wilson's play "Ma Rainey's Black Bottom," the third in his award-winning Pittsburgh Cycle chronicling African American life in the twentieth century. In the play, Ma is in a conversation with a man named Levee about the nature of the blues:

> Ma: White folks don't understand about the blues. They hear it come out, but they don't know how it got there. They don't understand that's life's way of talking. You don't sing to feel better. You sing 'cause that's a way of understanding life.

Levee: That's right.

Ma: You get that understanding and you done got a grip on life to where you can hold your head up and go on and see what else life got to offer. The blues help you to get out of the bed in the morning. You get up knowing you ain't alone. There's something else out there in the world. Something's been added by that song. This be an empty world without the blues. I take that emptiness and try and fill it up with something.[63]

In response, Levee suggests that the blues are sung in church too, sometimes. We can only imagine that Ma sang a sort of blues in church when at the end of her life she joined Friendship Baptist in Columbus. But her young piano protégé, Georgia Tom Dorsey, made the connection between the blues and the church much more directly.

Georgia Tom Dorsey

Recently transplanted in Atlanta from rural Villa Rica in Carroll County, Georgia, eleven-year-old Thomas Dorsey dropped out of school. After poor but happy early years in the city, he quickly grew discouraged by the struggles of urban poverty and racism–poor clothing, no shoes, and constant teasing at school for his dark complexion. He took up with other young boys on Decatur Street, the vibrant heart of the black business district in Atlanta. Hanging about the famous 81 Theater, he eventually got the chance to sell popcorn during intermissions, a job that allowed him to see the entertainers coming through. The music, always a part of his life before moving to Atlanta, now grabbed hold and did not let him go. Learning to play piano was all he could think about, and he idolized the players, especially Ed Butler, the main pianist at the 81.

Dorsey's father, Thomas, was a Baptist preacher educated at Atlanta Baptist (later Morehouse) College, and his mother, Etta, was a singer and keyboardist. Despite economic troubles that included years preaching revivals, subsistence farming, and, at their most desperate, sharecropping, the family shared a home rooted in faith and music. Dorsey was exposed to the old spirituals and hymns and to shape-note singing at Mount Prospect Baptist Church in Villa Rica, and he was exposed to the blues when his guitar-playing uncle occasionally visited. While these modes of music all influenced him, it was "moaning" that most marked his emotional memory.

> That moan . . . is just about known only to the black folk. Now I've heard them sing like this when I was a boy in churches, and that kind of singing would stir the churches up more so than one of those fast hymns or one of those hymns they sang out of the book.[64]

This moan connects to the feeling at the heart of Dorsey's great work, melding the blues and the gospels. As Dorsey biographer Michael Harris argues, it was not merely a style but an idea that was at the heart of Dorsey's greatness. The idea of the blues as a feeling was at the center of his music, and his marriage of this feeling to gospel music accounts for how he changed music history.[65]

A growing family and depressed cotton prices led to the Dorsey family's desperate move to Atlanta in pursuit of a better life. These early years in Atlanta saw both Thomas and Etta working, neither connected to a church, and the music of the streets became the catechism for young Tom. While he could never play their old pump organ as a child (he couldn't reach the pedals), he now returned from nights at the 81 to plunk out a tune he'd heard till he had it by heart.[66] Soon he was able to play the blues for neighborhood parties and developed a reputation as a popular entertainer. While he wanted to break into playing the theaters, he learned he'd have to read music to accompany the traveling acts and their varying musical styles. After a failed attempt at formal lessons from Mrs. Graves on the cultured west side of Atlanta's black community, Dorsey sent away for mail order books on musical notation and taught himself.

Dorsey's successful efforts at self-improvement taught him more than note reading; he also saw his limits as a performer in Atlanta. Already having participated in one of the century's great migrations (from rural life to the city), he, like many others, fell under the sway of newspaper ads promising jobs in Chicago, along with freedom from the constant racism of southern life. Arriving there with tens of thousands of others in the years before World War I, Dorsey jumped into the thriving music scene only to discover the same class divide between trained and untrained musicians. He found outlets for playing but again sought to improve himself by enrolling at the Chicago School of Composition and Arranging. Still, jazz had become the coin of the music scene, and the country blues Dorsey played did not lend themselves to the more desirable gigs at larger clubs and theaters. While he struggled along, playing Prohibition-era parties where the blues more readily fit the mood and clientele, the climate was shifting as a result of the recording industry.

In the early 1920s, Perry Bradford, a New York pianist and songwriter, convinced OKeh Records to record a "colored girl" named Mamie Smith. Her first record sold decently, but her second, "Crazy Blues," was a huge seller. That record changed the game, and blues was suddenly a hot commodity. Dorsey was playing gigs every night around Chicago, on the cusp of breaking through to another level of popularity, when he suffered his first nervous breakdown. His mother brought him home to Atlanta to recover, admonishing him to "serve the Lord, serve the Lord." Yet as soon as he was able, he was back in Chicago, working the ivories.

Soon after his return to Chicago, his uncle Joshua Dorsey, a pharmacist, invited him to the last session of the National Baptist Convention held in Chicago that September. It was the first moment in a decade-long journey for Dorsey in bringing together his lifelong connection to the blues and the church. During the closing, in part to sell the new Baptist hymnal *Gospel Pearls*, W. M. Nix sang "I Do, Don't You?" one of the twelve or so new gospel songs in the hymnal. It was not the song itself, but Nix's remarkable performance of it, that so captured Dorsey. He recalls that upon hearing it, "my inner-being was thrilled. My soul was in a deluge of divine rapture; my emotions were aroused; my heart was inspired to become a great singer and worker in the Kingdom of the Lord." Pondering what Nix had done to evoke such a powerful response, both for him and for the whole convention, Dorsey suggested that

> these turns and trills, he and a few others brought that into church music. Hymn singers, they couldn't pull this stuff in it. What he did, I wouldn't call it blues, but it had a touch of the blue note in there. Now that's the turn and the feeling that really made the gospel singers.[67]

It was, Dorsey continued, not only the blue note; but it was also the tempo, the slow style reminiscent of the "moanin'" of his childhood exposure to the spirituals. He threw himself into his newfound conviction, within a year publishing his first two sacred songs and taking a short-term position directing a choir at New Hope Baptist Church on Chicago's South Side. It was a first taste of spiritual resolution, playing blues "for the Lord," holding the congregation in the palm of his hand as he had often done in bars and at parties.

However, with the popularity of the blues on the rise again and the church job still only a volunteer position, he couldn't pass up an invitation to join Will Walker's Whispering Syncopators, his first professional gig, with a paycheck of forty dollars a week. He threw himself into the work, playing, composing, and publishing blues. Finally he broke through, with Monette Moore recording his "Muddy Water Blues" and the famous King Oliver recording "Riverside Blues." This attention helped get him the audition for Ma Rainey's tour in 1924 as leader of the Wildcats Jazz Band (detailed above).

After his marriage to Nettie Harper in 1925, she traveled with the band, working with Ma on her wardrobe. But as happened in 1921, Dorsey hit a wall. One night in the fall of 1926, while playing a show near Chicago, Dorsey felt a "slight unsteadiness" that grew until he couldn't play or do much of anything. He was down to 117 pounds and had to give up his position in the Wildcats. Nettie worked as a laundress for almost two years to help them get by, nursing him at night when she returned home.

After the 1926 "unsteadiness" and protracted illness, his sister-in-law finally convinced him to go to church with her to seek divine help. Dorsey recalls the events of that day in dramatic terms.

> It's hard to describe what happened. I thought more seriously about God than I had in many years, though I was a confessed believer and went to church. I shall never forget. The minister was Bishop H. H. Haley and he spoke gently and quietly to me: "Brother Dorsey, there is no reason for you to be looking so poorly and feeling so badly. The Lord has too much work for you to do to let you die."[68]

The bishop reached out and healed him, and from that moment on, Dorsey pledged to leave the blues career behind and serve the

Lord. He wrote his first gospel blues in response, called "If You See My Savior." Dorsey threw himself into the gospel blues business, seeking to sell his songs to the mainline African American churches that were his natural market. He met tremendous resistance, however, and was "thrown out of some of the best churches in the nation."[69] After decades of focus on education and sophistication, these churches hardly wanted to return to what influential AME bishop Daniel Payne derided as "cornfield ditties."[70] Dorsey learned that gospel blues was a hard sell.

Struggling financially to get his new gospel music publishing venture off the ground, Dorsey gave in to one last fling with the blues. Tampa Red Whittaker visited him one night with a lyric titled, "It's Tight Like That," a song with an obvious sexual double entendre. To the proposal that he write the music, Dorsey replied, "I don't do that music anymore." Whittaker said, "But there's big money in it if it clicks."[71] And Dorsey, sorry for the years Nettie had washed laundry to sustain them, and chagrined at the poor state of their furnishings and clothing, gave in. The song was written that day and recorded the next. The first royalty check was huge: $2,400.19. Dorsey "rushed home, gave [his] wife a couple hundred dollars, then took her down to an exclusive vogue shop. There [he] bought her some new clothes in appreciation."[72] Georgia Tom and Tampa Red recorded over sixty songs in the next couple of years, making plenty of money. But Dorsey never felt good about it, knowing he'd again broken his promise to work only "for the Lord."

Not long after his return to blues playing, the bank with all his savings failed and Dorsey lost all of his money. Nettie commented at the time that he had broken his promise to write only sacred music and that "God was displeased and suffered you to lose it all in the bank crash."[73] Again, Dorsey pledged to answer the call to dedicate himself to gospel songs only. The event perhaps most responsible for his ability to finally honor this pledge came after he found singers to perform his gospel blues songs, thus publicizing them in the churches. When Mrs. Willie Mae Fisher sang "If You See My Savior" at the 1930 National Baptist Convention meeting in Chicago, it brought down the assembly, and friends searched out Dorsey to set up a stand selling sheet music. He sold four thousand copies of the music at the convention alone, and soon after he received an invitation to form a gospel choir for Ebenezer Baptist. His showmanship and charismatic choir packed the church's services with the throngs of those recently arrived from southern states. In 1932, after Dorsey overwhelmed the congregation with a performance of his Ebenezer choir at the historic Pilgrim Baptist Church, Dr. J. C. Austin promptly recruited Dorsey to become director of music. He remained in that position for the rest of his life.

One more tragic moment awaited Dorsey, an event that in some profound sense sealed his merger of the blues and gospel at the most moving and human level. Later in 1932, Dorsey was invited to play a revival in St. Louis. Nettie was near the end of her pregnancy, and Dorsey promised her a "present" when he returned. He thought about not going, and even forgot his music bag, returning thirty miles to retrieve it quietly from their bedroom where Nettie was sleeping. The second night of the revival, Dorsey got a telegram.

> I opened it, and it read, "Your wife just died. Come home." I couldn't finish the gig. Finally I got home to Chicago the next morning and I found it all true, they'd never moved the body. And that chilled me, killed me off, I wanted to go back to the blues. But after putting my wife away, the baby in the same casket, I went to the old Poro College, in the music room there, Mr. Frye and I, just browsing over the keys, and seemingly the words like drops of water from a crevice in a rock above seemed to drop in line with me on the piano, "Precious Lord, take my hand, lead me on, let me stand, I'm tired, I'm weak, I'm worn. Through the storm, through the night, lead me on to the light, take my hand, Precious Lord, lead me home."[74]

Whereas until this point, Michael Harris points out, Dorsey "had only been able to cower away from sorrow in his gospels, he had always been able to cry out about it in his blues." Blues was, Dorsey always said, "a good man or woman, feeling bad." With "Precious Lord," Dorsey finally "allowed himself to wail, to get 'lowdown,' to purge—rather than just soothe—his grief."[75]

Dorsey saw a profound connection between the blues and church, rooted as they both are in what it means to be human, to cry out in the depths of our being in response to the circumstances of life:

I seen women in the audience jump up, so touched–guess a good
man had left them, left them cold or something like that–jump
up like you shouting in church. . . . Whatever it is that touches
them, they jump up and wring and shout just like we would in
church. It gets low-down. Now what we call low-down in blues
doesn't mean that it's dirty or bad or something like that. It gets
down into the individual to set him on fire, dig him up or dig her
up way down there 'til they come out with an expression verbally.
If they're in church, they say, "Amen." If they're in the blues, they
say, "Sing it now."[76]

Whether about a jilted lover or about the Creator, Dorsey claimed,
the music is a vehicle for "the same feeling, a grasping of the heart."
During those dark days of 1932 after Nettie's death, the only truth
that seemed real was this grasping of the heart that reached out
desperately for a hand to hold. "Precious Lord" was to become
among the most important gospel songs ever written, helping an
entire nation to mourn at the death of Martin Luther King Jr. and
at countless other times of trouble, large and small.[77]

SINGING THE TRUTH

Let's pause now to pull the threads of the chapter together. A key
point emerging from this study of the blues leads us away from
the characterization of the blues as "the devil's music" and to
an understanding of the blues as "secular spirituals." The key to
this shared arc of meaning between the blues and spirituals is the
struggle to speak the truth of life's loves and sorrows. Only through
the delight of desire and love do we find our hearts torn apart by
betrayal. This range of life's experience set before the hearer, and
before the Lord, draws powerfully on the blues. It can be both a
"feelin' " and a musical style rooted in Dorsey's "turns and trills,"
the deep "moanin' " Ma Rainey brought to her evocation of sorrow,
the profound sensitivity to the human condition with which Billie
Holiday tells you something about the pain of life.

While Dorsey and Rainey felt an internal "prodigal son/daugh-
ter" struggle that led them to eventually trade the blues for a life in
the church, the pressure to give up the blues had more to do with
the rigidity of what Jon Michael Spencer called the "European

Protestant" sacred–secular split than with the African religious sensibilities that understood the interconnection of body and soul, sexuality and spirituality, faith and doubt, love and betrayal. They all likely agreed with bluesman Henry Townsend, whom I quoted above as arguing, "Some people think that the blues is something that is evil–I don't. If the blues is delivered in the truth, which most of them are, if I sing the blues and tell the truth, what have I done? What have I committed? I haven't lied."[78] Dorsey, at his best, understood that the blues can be used for good or ill, just as gospel can. Either way, he seemed to say that on the one hand, one can stray from seeking the truth and laying it out before the Lord. On the other hand, one can reach deep down and draw out that "low-down feelin'," which come out as "wordless sighs, our aching groans" when we lack the words.[79]

The same might be said for rock and roll, the child of the blues. Its roots lie in the earthy spirituality of the blues, seeking to tell the truth about life, to sing sorrow and joy straight with no chaser (as the title to a classic Thelonious Monk jazz tune puts it). Bono captures this reality and helps us make the transition to the next chapter, which offers a hermeneutic of Scripture's cries. This hermeneutic unfolds "the blues in Scripture." As one who has drunk deeply from the well of the blues tradition, Bono describes what matters most to him in art and faith:

> The most important element in painting a picture, writing a song, making a movie, whatever, is that it is *truthful*, a version of the truth as you see it. Rock 'n roll, and the blues, they're truthful. It says in the Scriptures, "Know the truth, and the truth will set you free." . . . The blues is the truth of their own experience. In the Psalms of David, there is this powerful wailing against God. You know, "You call yourself God!" and "Where are you when I need you?" The psalms of David *are* the blues, and I get great comfort from that."[80]

In seeking to connect the blues to the Psalms, the cries of popular music to the cries of Scripture, we begin our next chapter.

4

CRIES

Help, God—the bottom has fallen out of my life!
Master, hear my cry for help!
Listen hard! Open your ears!
Listen to my cries for mercy.

—Psalm 130:1–2

As I begin this chapter, let me pause briefly to take stock of where
the argument has gotten to thus far. You might, in fact, have missed
that an argument is being made at all. The strategy has been to
tell stories of these pop culture artists in order to make an argument by example rather than offer propositions that I must defend.
Chapter 1 describes orientations to faith and life that avoid brokenness and suffering in the name of a God of righteousness and
blessing. Chapters 2 and 3, on Leonard Cohen and on the blues,
invite us to face life's struggles and sorrows, making sense by living through them instead of avoiding them. These chapters argue
against a popular understanding of Christianity that places brokenness and suffering against God, thereby implicitly (and sometimes
explicitly) understanding suffering to be a result of weak faith or

75

even of sin. In chapters 5 and 6 I delve much more deeply into the cultural power and systematic logic of such positions and offer a clear alternative. Already the argument made through engagement with Cohen's broken songs and with the cries of the blues shows that in avoiding suffering and brokenness, we lose the very ability to speak truthfully about our lives and thus to acknowledge the places where God is at work in us.

In sketching these stories of poets and singers who know broken-ness and suffering, I hope, of course, you are drawn in, that you say, *yes, that rings true; I know life is like that.* We know the deep truth of life is never pure beauty, never simple happiness. Somehow, as Don Saliers hauntingly puts it, terror and beauty exist together in the midst of life's brokenness.[1] As Cohen so aptly wrote, "there is a crack in everything, that's how the light gets in." This is not so much a description of how things ought to be as it is a description of how things actually are.

As I said in the introduction and will describe more fully below, certain theologies ask us to speak of our lives in ways that are not wholly truthful, that mislead us about who we are, what the world is like, and how God acts toward us. The previous two chapters opened up the question of how we can speak honestly about the deepest truths of our lives, including most profoundly the pain and injustice we experience, the spaces of abandonment and sorrow we feel, and the longing for healing and reconciliation we desire. These cries of the heart draw us in because of their raw emotion, and because in them we find ways of speaking truthfully about our own lives in community before God.

In this chapter, then, I turn to an interpretation of Scripture that shows these "cries of the heart" to be a key theme of the Bible, a way to make sense of God's relation to the world and to each of us. This chapter fits at the center of the book because here I make the case that the cries we make from the brokenness of our lives are at the heart of Scripture's promises about life and salvation. The Bible is not a place to turn in an effort to avoid brokenness and find purity and blessing. To be sure, passages of blessing and joy can be found; unfortunately they too often serve as the fodder fueling ide-ologies of prosperity and blessing operating across the globe today.[2] One example: Bruce Wilkinson's bestselling *The Prayer of Jabez: Breaking through to the Blessed Life* amounts to a meditation on the promise of prosperity taken from two verses (1 Chron. 4:9–10).[3] But the more profound and more central strand of the Bible teaches that it is out of identification with suffering that the character of God as redeemer becomes clear. Such a shape for the divine life offers not optimism about our prospects for being good and receiving blessings (à la Wilkinson). Rather, it offers a hope that even in the worst of circumstances we are not abandoned. God is there in our midst, fully identifying with our plight, and working to open new possibilities for life.

WISDOM CRIES

One of the most provocative interpretations of the theme of "cries" in Scripture comes from theologian David Ford, especially in his recent work on Christian wisdom. He found the prevalence and centrality of cries surprising as he searched the biblical texts for an understanding of wisdom. The more he searched for Christian wisdom, he writes,

> the more I have been struck by its core connection with cries: the cries for wisdom and the cries by the personified biblical wisdom; cries within and outside scripture that arise from the intensities of life–in joy, suffering, recognition, wonder, bewilderment, gratitude, expectation, or acclamation; and cries of people for what they most desire–love, justice, truth, goodness, compassion, children, health, food and drink, education, security, and so on. Christian wisdom is discerned within earshot of such cries, and is above all alert to the cries of Jesus.[4]

In showing how Jesus himself claims to be a "child of wisdom," Ford draws extensively from Luke's Gospel and the Acts of the Apostles to show the centrality of wisdom's cries. Through this reading of Jesus's life, Ford is able to lift up a central aspect of our own lives, as we too desire wisdom in our concern for life lived fully and faithfully.

Desire for God is a central theme for Ford, and it is rooted in the biblical persona of Wisdom herself as she cries out her invitation to all to come partake of her gifts of truth, to feast at her table of insight (Proverbs 9). Such a perspective sets up the fundamental scriptural reality that "the cry goes first to God."[5] The cries in Scripture are, Ford argues, elicited and relational, and might be described as a *vita passiva*.[6] This Latin term, meaning "the passive life," might sound quite countercultural, but without it one hardly understands Scripture and the central place of cries within it. Such language of "the passive life" points to the ways we are dependent on gifts for our very life, but it also points to the many concrete circumstances of difficulty and suffering. On the deepest level, we speak of salvation as "given," and upon that good gift of God we are dependent in the most profound sense.

God desires a relationship, freely offering the wisdom present in his own life to the world. Yet this very gracious gift sets the stage for the most incredible rejections, and from the start, acts of violence follow. Proverbs begins with this paradox of wisdom and ignorance, gift and violent rejection: "Start with GOD—the first step in learning is bowing down to GOD" (1:7). Lady Wisdom, who was with God "well before Earth got its start" (8:22–23), stands on the street corner and cries out for all who "wallow in ignorance" to come to her. "Look, I'm ready to pour out my spirit on you, I'm ready to tell you all I know" (1:22–23). Yet, as the story goes, all the way back to Adam and Eve in the garden (Gen. 3), and their sons Cain and Abel in the fields (Gen. 4), humans have "turned a deaf ear" to wisdom's call (1:24).

Despite humanity's "turning a deaf ear," God sounds the primal call for the sake of the Earth. Lady Wisdom, here in the famous passage, calls out:

> Do you hear Lady Wisdom calling?
> Can you hear Madame Insight raising her voice?
> She's taken her stand at First and Main, at the busiest
>   intersection.
> Right in the city square where the traffic is thickest, she
>   shouts,
> "You—I'm talking to all of you, everyone out here on the
>   streets!" (Proverbs 8:1–4)

This invitation is to find life that is truly life, to enjoy something "better than all the trappings of wealth" (8:11). Such an invitation is for a way of living "on Righteous Road—that's where I walk—at the intersection of Justice Avenue, handing out life to those who love me, filling their arms with life, armloads of life!" (8:20–21). This life is the desire of God for creation. It is the promise for which God's people cry out in longing. And it is out of God's desire for the life of every living thing that such cries, when they sound forth from the depths of sorrow and despair, are heard.

OUT OF SUFFERING

The exodus story is the primal story of the people of Israel, one that helps make sense of a God who identifies with and acts amid suffering. While the creation stories that mark the Bible's beginnings in the book of Genesis have their great line, "In the beginning," the central creation story, the creation of the "people of God," is Exodus. One might say that the ancient stories of Genesis constitute the "backstory" that helps to make intelligible this foundational story of Israel's deliverance from slavery under Pharaoh.

As Exodus unfolds, we see briefly how the book gestures back through the stories of Genesis to the promise and power of the creation stories. Here's how the book begins:

> These are the names of the Israelites who went to Egypt with Jacob, each bringing his family members: Reuben, Simeon, Levi, and Judah, Issachar, Zebulun, and Benjamin, Dan and Naphtali, Gad and Asher. Seventy persons in all generated by Jacob's seed. Joseph was already in Egypt. Then Joseph died, and all his brothers–that whole generation. But the children of Israel kept on reproducing. They were very prolific–a population explosion in their own right–and the land was filled with them. (Exod. 1:1–7)

Walter Brueggemann, an esteemed scholar of the Old Testament, likes to quip that it took a cry to get God into the book of Exodus.[7] Yet Terence Fretheim has been eloquent and persuasive in showing the presence of God the Creator right from the beginning, though God is not *named* in Exodus until the end of chapter 2.[8] In recalling the Joseph story, the author notes the work of God's hand. It recalls a redemption story, not just of Joseph's own life saved from the pit and slavery but also of a whole people saved from starvation. Fretheim also convincingly connects the prolific nature of the children of Israel to the command to be fruitful in Genesis 1:28 and 9:1. This given and renewed promise of fruitfulness is being fulfilled, and so, Fretheim argues, the book of Exodus opens by framing the dramatic redemption story it tells within the ongoing creative purposes of God.

Into this opening a further dramatic element is added: "A new king came to power in Egypt who didn't know Joseph" (1:8). This simple statement bears unpacking, for the meaning goes far beyond not knowing *Joseph*. It is a way to say this new king knows nothing of the God whose creative work extends from the beginning through the remarkable story of Joseph to a promised future of blessing for all nations. And this new king, unsettled by the obvious power of this people and its God, succumbs to his fears and quickly turns to oppressive policy.

> So they organized them into work-gangs and put them to hard labor under gang-foremen. They built the storage cities Pithom and Rameses for Pharaoh. But the harder the Egyptians worked them the more children the Israelites had–children everywhere! The Egyptians got so they couldn't stand the Israelites and treated them worse than ever, crushing them with slave labor. They made them miserable with hard labor–making bricks and mortar and back-breaking work in the fields. They piled on the work, crushing them under the cruel workload. (Exod. 1:11–14)

Whether this story is taken as historical or symbolic, or some mixture of the two, its power and truth could not be clearer from the language itself. The writers of Exodus use the Hebrew term for service (*'ābad*) nearly a hundred times, and later in the story the term is used for the service implied by worship.[9] Here, the comparison goes, the Israelites must serve Pharaoh, but later they freely serve Yahweh. The passage sets up the conflict between powerful rulers, between two sorts of demands for allegiance and two visions of life. With Pharaoh, Egypt demands the subjugation of the Israelites. Their life demands death-dealing, miserable labor; yet even there, in the midst of such antilife servitude, the Israelites prosper, so much so that Pharaoh turns to desperate measures–aiming to kill them directly rather than indirectly through deprivation and brutal work.

Pause for a moment to consider with whom you most identify, for the story implicitly asks our allegiance too. The story "reads" us. In her passionate work *Set Them Free: The Other Side of Exodus*, Laurel Dykstra argues that most Christians in the wealthy countries of the North Atlantic read this story and align themselves with ancient Israel.[10] "We, too, were slaves in Egypt," people are tempted to say. "We, too, shouted, 'Old Pharaoh, let my people go.'" Songs that say as much are a regular feature of vacation Bible schools and church camps, youth retreats and popular spirituals. Yet, Dykstra reminds us, those who live in a country such as the twenty-first-century United States have far more in common with Pharaoh's Egypt than with the Israelites.

It is instructive to follow along as Dykstra unpacks the "Egyptian traits" of life in North America: violence, slavery, genocide, and deceit. Historically, slavery and violence commingled in the agricultural system of the United States, and sharecropping continued this legacy of exploitation. Even today, similar dynamics are at work among those within and beyond our borders who toil in unjust conditions to produce cheap goods, including food and clothing. The mere existence of the fair trade and sweatshop-free movements testify to this reality. Genocide, too, is woven into our history, both with the Native peoples of North America, who were decimated by disease and war, and the African peoples, who were torn from their homeland and subjugated for our nation's economic prosperity. Both groups still disproportionately suffer poverty, imprisonment, and early death compared to the general population. In addition, we have, despite our incredible power as a nation, stood aside while genocide took place around the world, Darfur being only the most recent example. Lying and deceit are necessary to maintain the myth we tell ourselves to preserve the sense of our own moral honor. To tell the truth about our history and current circumstances, as the late historian Howard Zinn taught us to do in his *People's History of the United States*, evokes the cry of "Traitor!" from some quarters. Yet our best leaders, such as Abraham Lincoln and Martin Luther King Jr., have shown us that it is only through truth-telling that we become the moral people we aspire to be.

Truth-telling, however, does not cut evenly across all situations. Theologian Andrew Root, drawing on Dietrich Bonhoeffer, has argued that telling the naked truth can often be harmful and nothing other than a power play under the cover of morality.[11] For instance, what if Miep and Jan Gies had not twisted the truth again and again to protect the Frank family hiding in their house in Amsterdam? In the end, someone did tell the truth, an action resulting in the deaths of everyone the couple had concealed except Otto Frank. The story could be multiplied many times over, and most circumstances of this sort are unknown to us because the stories died with the persecuted. So one might say that those who bear the "traits of Egypt" have a somewhat different responsibility to truth than those whose necks are under the boot of oppression.

Sensitivity to the sides we claim as we read Exodus heightens our sensitivity to the sides claimed by the characters in the story—whether explicitly or implicitly. We paused in the story just at the point of Pharaoh's decision to give up on indirect methods of killing Israelites by oppressive labor. Now he sets in motion his plan to kill them directly. He meets with "midwives to the Hebrews" and tells them that when they attend births, they must kill the boys and let the girls live. We never learn the name of the king, but the midwives are named: Shiprah and Puah. They are, we shall see, examples of the complexity of truth-telling. Because "the midwives feared God," they do not follow the king's orders; they let the all the children live. When summoned before the king and charged with insurrection, they claim the Hebrew women are "not like the Egyptian women" and give birth before the midwife comes to them. Renita Weems describes their actions beautifully:

> The midwives don't lie, they simply do not tell the whole truth. It is the conventional weapon of the powerless, especially women in the Old Testament, against those in power: the weapon of deception where the "truth" is not defined by the powerful but becomes the priority of the underclass to interpret and shape according to their own reality. The refusal to tell the "truth" becomes tantamount to the refusal to obey.[12]

God rewards them, and Pharaoh apparently doesn't punish them. However, he gives up on intermediaries and simply orders every newborn Hebrew boy thrown into the Nile.

While it has often been assumed that the midwives were Israelites, Laurel Dykstra has suggested that there are reasons to imagine them as Egyptians too.[13] The king obviously knows them and expects them to do his evil bidding. They have knowledge of how Egyptian women give birth. And the text presents the fact that the midwives "feared God" as a surprise. Viewing them this way does make our proximity to them challenging; they are, one might say, examples of a distinctly faith-based politics of civil disobedience. Their actions protest their privileged proximity to Pharaoh. Remarkably, they also prefigure God's own action by opening their ears and hearts to the plight of the suffering. While the divine king ought to be the one with wisdom, the midwives emerge as the ones who honor God, a posture that echoes a common theme in Scripture: "Start with GOD–the first step in learning is bowing down to GOD; only fools thumb their noses at such wisdom and learning" (Prov. 1:7). Their wisdom leads them to compassion, to the capacity to hear the newborn cries, and to honor life rather than destroy it. They prefigure how God will act in this story, and through their actions God is active in the same creative and life-giving ways God has been present and known in the past.

Pharaoh refuses to tell the truth of his cruelty and oppression, to intuit the wisdom to honor life (and implicitly the God of life) as the midwives had done, and to compassionately hear the cries of the suffering of the people. We are not here told of the hardening of Pharaoh's heart, as we are later in the story. In fact, we hear nothing of the king's response to the midwives' actions except that it leads him to the desperate policy of direct murder of all newborn boys (an act we will return to below in discussing Herod and Jesus). It is in the context of this genocidal threat that we hear the story of another incredible act–of disobedience to Pharaoh and allegiance to God–in the actions of the king's daughter in response to a little baby's cries.

> A man from the family of Levi married a Levite woman. The woman became pregnant and had a son. She saw there was something special about him and hid him. She hid him for three months. When she couldn't hide him any longer she got a little basket-boat made of papyrus, waterproofed it with tar and pitch, and placed the child in it. Then she set it afloat in the reeds at the edge of the Nile.

The baby's older sister found herself a vantage point a little way off and watched to see what would happen to him. Pharaoh's daughter came down to the Nile to bathe; her maidens strolled on the bank. She saw the basket-boat floating in the reeds and sent her maid to get it. She opened it and saw the child–a baby crying! Her heart went out to him. She said, "This must be one of the Hebrew babies."

Then his sister was before her: "Do you want me to go and get a nursing mother from the Hebrews so she can nurse the baby for you?"

Pharaoh's daughter said, "Yes. Go." The girl went and called the child's mother.

Pharaoh's daughter told her, "Take this baby and nurse him for me. I'll pay you." The woman took the child and nursed him.

After the child was weaned, she presented him to Pharaoh's daughter who adopted him as her son. She named him Moses (Pulled-Out), saying, "I pulled him out of the water." (Exod. 2:1–10)

Much has been made of the symbolism in this story prefiguring the coming saving action of God. Moses embodies Israel's circumstances of suffering and miraculous saving from the waters. Yet this dynamic prefiguring of the story of Israel in the experience of baby Moses has a stunning parallel. It is, after all, the king's daughter who hears the cry, has compassion, rescues the baby, and makes him her own. This daughter of Pharaoh is the one who prefigures the actions of God! She very likely knows of the edict of the king; upon seeing the baby she says, "This must be one of the Hebrew babies." That she was in proximity to the child's cries, heard them, and had compassion allowed her an opportunity to move against Pharaoh in her own modest way, subverting the horror without fully knowing her place in the unfolding story.

Yet we know that Moses grew up in Pharaoh's household. We might assume that he remained somewhat sheltered and yet knew his identity, knew the secret of his subversive place within the structures of power. Such a sketch makes sense of why as a young man Moses went to see his people for himself and there beheld the wretchedness of their forced labor. His murderous act when faced with an Egyptian beating a Hebrew slave figures in the story as a means to have him called by God in the wilderness. Yet, in that moment of flashing anger, we can see the dramatic tension between Moses's privilege and his association with the suffering of his people. Such an act of violence also prefigures God's own violent actions to free the Israelites from bondage a few chapters later.[14]

Moses flees, fearful that his deed of violence is known. As the story unfolds, we learn that his fears are borne out: "Pharaoh heard about it and tried to kill Moses" (2:15). It is in his first wilderness sojourn that Moses, tending sheep for his father-in-law's flocks, meets God at the holy mountain of Horeb. We could explore many angles of interest in this famous story, but my interest here is God's message to Moses as a means to understand God's character, echoing the character of the midwives and Pharaoh's daughter. In setting up this story of Moses's fateful encounter with God on the mountain, the narrator's voice intervenes to say the king of Egypt had died and that the Israelites' groans and cries of suffering rose up to God. "God," the narrator tells us, "remembered his covenant with Abraham, with Isaac, and with Jacob. God saw what was going on with Israel. God understood" (2:24–25). So when Moses does come face-to-face with God, so to speak, in the theophany of the burning bush, it is no surprise what God has to say. In every way we have been prepared to understand God as the direct opposite of Pharaoh.

> GOD said, "I've taken a good, long look at the affliction of my people in Egypt. I've heard their cries for deliverance from their slave masters; I know all about their pain. And now I have come down to help them, pry them loose from the grip of Egypt, get them out of that country and bring them to a good land with wide-open spaces, a land lush with milk and honey, the land of the Canaanite, the Hittite, the Amorite, the Perizzite, the Hivite, and the Jebusite.
>
> "The Israelite cry for help has come to me, and I've seen for myself how cruelly they're being treated by the Egyptians. It's time for you to go back: I'm sending you to Pharaoh to bring my people, the People of Israel, out of Egypt." (Exod. 3:7–10)

A Pharaoh arose in Egypt who "didn't know Joseph" (1:8). Yet God knows Joseph's descendants and knows their pain. Pharaoh again and again refuses to hear the cries of oppression and the entreaties of Moses to let the Israelites go. God, like the midwives and the king's daughter, hears the Israelites' cries and responds. And it is instructive that despite the dramatic unfolding of events to follow, God does not act by fiat. Rather, God depends on human partners, as was the case with the midwives and with Pharaoh's daughter. Moses, and soon his siblings, Aaron and Miriam, are drawn into the action as God seeks to pry the Israelites from the grip of Egypt.

The unfolding of the fight for freedom leads to cries of horror from the Egyptians, and it is a difficult challenge to say how a God who hears the cries of the suffering responded to *those* cries, especially when those cries were of Egypt's own innocent children slain on the historic night of the Passover, celebrated to this day by Jews and Christians. I cannot resolve the crisis of meeting God as both compassionate and violent in this story. At the very least it requires noting that the Israelites' escape—a tale of their cries of terror turned to shouts of joy—comes at an incredible cost. Egypt's loss inspires a "lament such as has never been and never will be again" (Exod. 11:6). Here we come face-to-face with the complexity of Yahweh, something I will return to below with the lens Jesus gives us to see God as both hearer of cries and present in the midst of the suffering itself, crying out.

ECHOES OF EXODUS

The Exodus story becomes a paradigm for Israel's self-understanding as faithful, as God's holy nation. Again and again, we see the admonition to remember Egypt and to act accordingly:

> Don't abuse or take advantage of strangers; you, remember, were once strangers in Egypt.
>
> Don't mistreat widows or orphans. If you do and they cry out to me, you can be sure I'll take them most seriously; I'll show my anger and come raging among you with the sword, and your wives will end up widows and your children orphans. (Exod. 22:21–24)

Whatever we say in the end about the portrayal of God's violence, a biblical case can be made for a God who does not countenance abuse or oppression and who hears the cries of the poor and responds. Likewise, the Scriptures remain almost entirely skeptical of "Egypt-like" social orders. One can see this in the discussion in 1 Samuel 8, where Israel declares that it wants a king, like other nations have. Samuel, an old man by this time, has little patience for what he sees as a wholly problematic request. Listing a litany of burdens, taxes, and costs, he wraps up his speech with this: "You'll end up no better than slaves. The day will come when you will cry in desperation because of this king you so much want for yourselves. But don't expect GOD to answer" (1 Sam. 8:17–18).

Indeed, much of the story of God and God's chosen can be told in the space between cries and God's responses. While the elite's descent into debauchery and idolatry at the expense of the poor leads to prophetic denunciations of Israel's kings and, ultimately, exile as a means of punishment, such action is always portrayed as restorative. After fierce denunciations, Isaiah is able to point to the God who waits to be gracious. He writes, "Oh yes, people of Zion, citizens of Jerusalem, your time of tears is over. Cry for help and you'll find it's grace and more grace. The moment he hears, he'll answer" (Isa. 30:19). Some chapters later, Isaiah's voice crying out in the wilderness announced this return of God's mercy. The announcement is a harbinger of the Messiah and a ready script for a later prophet, John the Baptist, to steal. Isaiah shouts out, "Prepare for God's arrival! Make the road straight and smooth, a highway fit for our God. Fill in the valleys, level off the hills, smooth out the ruts, clear out the rocks. Then God's bright glory will shine and everyone will see it. Yes. Just as God has said" (Isa. 40:3–5).

While the theme of cries of pain and joy is picked up and echoed throughout Scripture, it is perhaps nowhere as profound as in "Israel's prayer book," the book of Psalms. There we find the full range of the life of creation, held before God in praise and protests, joyful noise and sorrowful lament. Yet Psalm 3:4 captures the core pattern that echoes the exodus experience and resounds through so many psalms: "With all my might I shout up to God, His answers thunder from the holy mountain."[15] The suffering ones at times are portrayed as trusting: "I waited and waited and waited for GOD. At last he looked; finally he listened" (40:1). Other times the voice of the suffering is much more demanding, crying out in desperate anger at the delay of God's response: "Get up, God! Are you going to sleep all day? Wake up! Don't you care what happens to us?" (44:23–24).

At times it seems that there will be no response at all to the cries of the suffering one who feels totally abandoned: "You made lover and neighbor alike dump me; the only friend I have left is Darkness" (88:18). The experience of total abandonment echoing in the Psalms leads us straight to the Gospels, where, the evangelists say, we find these exact cries of lament on Jesus's lips in his moment of deepest suffering and, mysteriously, deepest identification with the world: the cross. To understand this more fully, we'll turn now to an examination of the interplay between Psalm 22 and Matthew's account of Jesus's life, death, and resurrection.

THE "LOUD CRY" FROM THE CROSS

The cry of despair from the cross (Matt. 27:46) embodies all the cries that pervaded Jesus's life and ministry. Stretching from Mary's own cries at his birth (Matt. 1:25) through the joyful cries of the women in telling the disciples the angel's news that he had been raised from the dead (Matt. 28:8), these cries deepen our understanding of God's character as the one who hears our cry. Matthew's telling of the Jesus story explicitly makes these connections between ancient and present cries of suffering and God's response. Viewed as a "Jewish-Christian" Gospel, Matthew works at the intersection of the Jewish scriptures and his understanding of their fulfillment in Jesus. He does this as a pastoral move, working to bring together a Jewish-Christian community in the aftermath of the destruction of the Jerusalem temple in AD 70.[16]

The beginning of Matthew's Gospel immediately shows a deep connection between ancient stories and Jesus. The first chapter tells the genealogy that ties Jesus directly to David and, before him, those who first sojourned in Egypt: Abraham, Isaac, and especially Jacob, along with his sons. The second chapter opens with a frightened, insecure, and cruel King Herod who hears that another king has been born. Herod hears of this new king through the Magi, non-Jews who have come from the east to pay homage. When Herod fails to con the Magi into directing him to the child, he resorts to direct means and orders the killing of all children in and around Bethlehem. These horrific actions recall an insecure and cruel Pharaoh whose effort to con the midwives failed, leading to genocidal policies with regard to the Hebrew children. Yet, by miraculous means, Jesus is saved from this murderous policy, just as Moses was. The very fact that Jesus flees to safety in Egypt gives away Matthew's ploy of reversals that portray Herod, the so-called king of the Jews, in the role of despised Pharaoh. The despised Pharaoh had to die before Moses could be commissioned and sent back to Egypt; Jesus, too, remained in Egypt until Herod died, only then returning with his family to settle in Nazareth, in Galilee.

Thus far, Matthew is stunningly successful in weaving threads of the ancient Scriptures and the experience of Jesus for the sake of his Jewish-Christian community. Moses the prophet, the heroic servant of God, offers a model for how to understand Jesus. Yet Matthew's task of weaving old and new becomes immeasurably harder when we pause to take stock of the rupture that must be accounted for: this same Moses-like figure must be rejected, suffer, and die. Christianity, writes Rowan Williams, "is born out of a struggle because it is born from men and women faced with the paradox of God's purpose made flesh in a dead and condemned man."[17] The story portrays real and painful tensions between those from the religious establishment who supported the legacy of Herod, ultimately rejecting Jesus as God's son, and those who cry out, "You are the Christ, the Son of the Living God" (Matt. 16:16).

The paradoxical rejection of God's anointed challenges the claim that he came from the very same Lord who heard Israel's cries in Egypt. This tension sets the context for Matthew's use of Psalm 22 at the end of the story. Matthew turns to this powerful lament psalm for help in making sense of this "strange God . . . who does not uncover his will in a straight line of development, but fully enters into a world of confusion and ambiguity and works in contradictions–the new covenant which both fulfills and radically alters the old, the Messianic age made real amid the suffering and failure of the present time."[18]

One can debate the likelihood of Jesus actually speaking the words of Psalm 22 from the cross. On the level of the story, Matthew (following Mark) crafted his versions of the death of Jesus with references to this powerful psalm. In the unfolding of the story, one might say, all the characters act "biblically" in that their actions seem to be scripted by the unfolding of events in Psalm 22. Yet many scholars view this convention for writing the story emerging from the early Christian community's memory of the actual "loud cry" of Jesus from the cross. Some have even suggested that it was common for Jews in times of adversity to quote this psalm. However, evidence of this is extremely thin. Another, stronger possibility lies in the use of such lament psalms in a *todah* ceremony, a gathering to celebrate a friend's deliverance, which recounts the suffering and confesses what God has done and giving thanks and praise. Bread (and possibly wine) played a role in such gatherings, adding credence to the idea that this kind of gathering of the disciples after the resurrection of Jesus gave shape to the early church's core interpretation of the death of Jesus on the cross (and its practice of Eucharist).

The allusions or direct quotations from Psalm 22 build through the last days of Jesus, culminating in the cry of abandonment from the cross that quotes directly from verse 1. In a fast-paced series of unfolding vignettes, Matthew describes the events from the Passover meal Jesus shared with the disciples, in which they held a last supper. Jesus retreated to pray in Gethsemane, where he was arrested and taken to appear before first the high priest and then Pilate. All the while, Matthew's reader observes the unraveling threads of his disciples' allegiance: Peter's denial and Judas's betrayal, and the disappearance of all but the women. As if echoing the key role women played in the story of the escape from Egypt, Matthew recounts, "There were also quite a few women watching from a distance, women who had followed Jesus from Galilee in order to serve him. Among them were Mary Magdalene, Mary the mother of James and Joseph, and the mother of the Zebedee brothers" (27:55–56).

Despite the continued presence of the women "from a distance," the cry of Jesus does come in the context of a cascade of abandonments: by his disciples (26:56), by the mocking soldiers (27:27–31), by the taunting bystanders (27:40–43), and finally even by the bandits who were crucified with him (27:44). Such mocking picks up Psalm 22:17–18: "They pin me down hand and foot, and lock me in a cage–a bag of bones in a cage, stared at by every passerby. They take my wallet and the shirt off my back, and then throw dice for my clothes." Indeed, Matthew tells us that the soldiers "whiled away the time by throwing dice for his clothes" (27:35). The taunting also echoes Psalm 22:7–8: "Everyone pokes fun at me; they make faces at me, they shake their heads: 'Let's see how God handles this one; since God likes him so much, let God help him!' " Here is the central moment in the charges against him, throwing back in the face of Jesus the very claim announced at his baptism, when "along with the Spirit, a voice: 'This is my Son, chosen and marked by my love, delight of my life' " (Matt. 3:17). This same claim comes at a crucial juncture in Jesus's ministry, when Peter blurts out his claim of Jesus as Messiah. As Jesus hangs on the cross, a crowd of religious leaders—chief priests, scribes, and elders—scoffed, "He saved others—he can't save himself! King of Israel, is he? Then let him get down from that cross. We'll all become believers then! He was so sure of God—well, let him rescue his 'Son' now—if he wants him! He did claim to be God's Son, didn't he?' Even the two criminals crucified next to him joined in the mockery" (Matt. 27:42–43).

In the midst of this mockery, under a darkness that fell over the whole land, "around mid-afternoon Jesus groaned out of the depths, crying loudly, 'Eli, Eli, lama sabachthani?' which means, 'My God, my God, why have you abandoned me?' " (Matt 27:46). While this is a wrenching moment, Matthew can connect deeply to the cries of the tradition: "God, God . . . my God! Why did you dump me miles from nowhere? Doubled up with pain, I call to God all the day long. No answer. Nothing. I keep at it all night, tossing and turning" (Ps. 22:1–2). By his turn to Psalm 22, however, Matthew's portrait of Jesus then also recalls by implication God's faithfulness in the past and on that basis points toward the fulfillment of the old in the experience of Jesus's life and death, *and* promises resurrection three days later. Psalm 22 begins with wrenching lament, yet already in the third verse the psalmist recalls the exodus experience as the very heart of faith. Doing so qualifies the sense of forsakenness from God announced in the opening cry (Jesus's own cry).

> And you! Are you indifferent, above it all, leaning back on the cushions of Israel's praise? We know you were there for our parents: they cried for your help and you gave it; they trusted and lived a good life. (Ps. 22:3–5)

Recalling this exodus experience also boldly claims God's character as the one who hears and responds, and expects no less of God in this present moment.

It doesn't seem to me a substantial matter whether one imagines that Jesus himself had this psalm on his lips. Or, as may be the case, his nonverbal cry of anguish led the early church community to draw upon this psalm for a description of its own experience of Jesus's dying. Both function within Matthew's Gospel to help the disciples not only to face the sorrowful lament but also to see its full horizon leading to God's decisive action in raising Jesus. The author of the psalm tenderly claims such a future (vv. 9–11) through recalling (again) the narrative world of the exodus, this time making explicit the connection between the midwives who save and God's own saving action:

> And to think you were midwife at my birth, setting me at my mother's breasts! When I left the womb you cradled me; since the moment of birth you've been my God. Then you moved far away and trouble moved in next door. I need a neighbor.

Such powerful and intimate connection is intended to portray the way God, unlike Pharaoh or Herod, is full of compassion and is moved to hear the cry and respond out of love. It is not a surprise, then, to come to the latter part of the psalm and find: "He has never let you down, never looked the other way when you were being kicked around. He has never wandered off to do his own thing; he has been right there, listening" (v. 24). Psalm 22 resolves in apocalyptic visions of even those who "sleep in the earth" bowing down before the Lord. Such an amazing vision both points to Jesus's own resurrection and gives background for Matthew's insertion in the story that "many bodies of believers asleep in their graves were raised" (27:52).

It is a painful irony that in Matthew's unfolding of the story, the chief priests and Pharisees are the ones who (gathered before Pilate) recall the words of Jesus, "After three days I will be raised" (27:62). Should this happen, these conspirators perceptively worried, "then we'll be worse off than before, the final deceit surpassing the first" (27:64). Presumably, the first deception was Jesus's "supposed" divine identity, the truth declared at his baptism but thrown back at him by these religious leaders in the taunts on the cross. Their worry about a "final deceit" shows how blinded they were to God's promises and power. All they could imagine happening was the disciples stealing his body and claiming he had been raised. They put too much faith in the disciples, who are in hiding, and not enough faith in God, whose actions are hidden from their eyes in plain sight.

When (again) the women appear in the story, they are at the tomb after the Sabbath at dawn, and an angel of the Lord appears to them, urging them not to be afraid and telling them, "I know you are looking for Jesus, the one they nailed to the cross. He is not here. He was raised, just as he said" (28:5–6). Had the leaders and disciples recalled the full trajectory of Israel's experience, as poetically rendered by Psalm 22, they could have (and at least the disciples would have) come to share the final word of praise: "As the word is passed along from parent to child. Babies not yet conceived will hear the good news–that God does what he says" (22:30b–31).

CONCLUSION

The slave now free; the criminal condemned to death now alive. These deep patterns at the heart of Scripture make a powerful claim about the relationship of our human brokenness and the cries that rise from the shards of our lives to the compassionate heart of God. By God's merciful response we know both who we are and who God is; we know how the world is and how it ought to be. Even more, the God we meet in these stories of human cries and divine response opens a way for us to see the reality of reconciled life. God who freed Israel, who raised Jesus from the dead, desires to make all creation whole, free, and new in the very midst of the mess that causes such suffering in the first place. Those who meet Jesus now live, as Rowan Williams puts it, "in and from the life of Jesus crucified and risen." The action of God to reconcile and make new does not erase the brokenness to which God is responding. Rather, God's actions point to the place of brokenness, to the location of the cry, as the sure place of God's presence and work. Rowan Williams again:

> The resurrection is that which points to the crucified as God's decisive manifestation. . . . The resurrection which sets free the mission of the church to reconcile, which creates reconciled lives, directs us to Calvary as an event which uncovers the truth: the

resilient, inexhaustible, demanding objectivity of what God and God's work is like. From now on, all that can be said of God's action in the past or the present must pass under the judgment of this fact.[19]

To simply boil it down to "this fact" feels too simple, I know. But what Williams is after is the way that Jesus's "loud cry" of abandonment signals a divine "no" to the forces of sin, evil, and violence that support their powerful reign in this life. God hears that cry and in the mystery of God's own life is "within" that cry. Therefore in raising Jesus from the dead, God took that brokenness and death into God's self, absorbed its power, and transformed its "no" to a cosmic and definitive "yes."[20]

God says "yes" to all that Jesus stood for, to be sure, as the one about whom John said, "Here he is, God's Passover Lamb! He forgives the sins of the world" (John 1:29). But more than that, God says "yes" to life in all its redeemed beauty and goodness. What is at stake, then, is not just Jesus's "loud cry" from the cross. What is at stake is the profound way this cry picks up all the cries that arise during his life and ministry. More than that, its cosmic character picks up all cries, from the cries of the exodus and exile to those of the psalmist and the prophets, from the moans of the blues singers and the broken ballads of the folksinger to the broken lives lived by you and me. The "fact" Williams claims as the central characteristic for understanding God's action is that God's resurrection "yes" to Jesus is in answer to all these cries summed up somehow in that one cry. Here, rooted in the witness of Scripture, we find much more than some simplistic "prayer of Jabez" that wishes for enlarged territory. Here we find a much more complicated wisdom to help us understand the work of God and the wound of grace.

PART II

5

GRACE AND KARMA

Is anyone crying for help? God is listening,
    ready to rescue you.
If your heart is broken, you'll find God right there;
      if you're kicked in the gut, he'll help you catch your breath.

                —Psalm 34:17–18

Sometimes coming face-to-face with suffering causes a reaction so visceral we can't do more than gasp, perhaps covering our mouth or averting our eyes to let it sink in. Such a situation unfolded on a warm day in early May 2009 at a playground in Albuquerque, New Mexico. A mother playing with her children spotted a shoe in the sand. Imagining some child had lost the shoe, she bent down to retrieve it and place it on a visible ledge for the searching parent to find later on. The shoe resisted her pull, however, and to her horror she discovered a dead boy buried in the sand.

It took more than a week for the mystery of what happened to surface. After circulating a sketch of the three-and-half-year-old toddler, the police received tips and arrested twenty-three-year-old Tiffany Toribio. As the horrible details unfolded, it became clear what a troubled young woman she was. Homeless, having been kicked out of her mother's house and a friend's apartment, running from an abusive boyfriend, and in deep despair about her prospects, she landed in the park at the playground. As her son, Tyruss, fell asleep in her arms, she held her hand over his face to suffocate him. Wracked by doubts, she stopped, did CPR to resuscitate him, but then smothered him again, burying his body in the sand under the play structure where he had fallen asleep in her arms. "Tiffany said that she did not want him to grow up with no one caring about him the same way she had grown up with no one caring about her," said Police Chief Ray Schultz.[1] She attempted suicide within twelve hours of her arrest.

As news of the story broke, responses were predictably strong. It was, one reporter wrote, "a crime so cold-blooded that neighbors struggled to comprehend it, and veteran officers became choked up."[2] Blogs and newspaper comment sections burned with condemnation. A particularly dramatic website, "People You'll See In Hell," had this to say:

> She committed a crime that is so heinous, so abominable, that we as thinking human beings have difficulty comprehending her actions. It is bad enough for a mother to suffocate her child, but to revive that child only to suffocate them again? That is pure unadulterated evil.

The post concluded with a poll: Does Tiffany Toribio deserve the fires of hell? Options were "Sure she does" and "No, she doesn't."

I voted partly so that I could see the results: 88 percent said she deserves hell. That I voted "no" is at the heart of the challenge this book offers in terms of how we understand God's relation to suffering and cries of all sorts. I can say, as a father, that the story breaks my heart, and I have a hard time fathoming the evil that grips a parent when she reaches the point of suffocating her own child. She committed an awful deed and deserved the consequences the law brought to bear. Yet reading reports of her circumstances did not add up to the easy labels of Tiffany as "crazy" or "evil," as many pundits and bloggers were quick to suggest. Rather, I wondered how she could have become so broken that she could have come to the point of envisioning the death of her son as a way forward in her life. Research on mothers killing their children is beginning to raise just such issues, showing that too often their circumstances include abuse and profound isolation from exactly those sources–both healthy networks of personal support and professional help–that could help prevent such horrible actions.[3]

Unfortunately, the tragic situation of Tiffany Toribio is not unique. Many–too many–families struggle with abandonment and abuse, and too many children bear the brunt of violence they neither understand nor deserve. And such family tragedy is only one sort of sorrow or struggle causing cries of despair today.[4] The brokenness described by poet-singers like Leonard Cohen and the unvarnished truth moaned in the blues are deeply connected to the way Scripture portrays human suffering and divine response. Yet the fact is that as people of faith, we too often fail to listen for and respond to the cries of suffering in culture generally and in pop music particularly. Too often, because of the horror of the situation, something like a belief in karma takes over our response. A sort of American Christianized version of karma–the idea that one's good or bad actions return good or bad, and thus people tend to get what they deserve–leads people to say, "She deserves the fires of hell." In fact, this often takes the seemingly innocuous form of a desire to keep such "bad" things far away from "good" people like us, to keep ourselves and our families "safe."

This book as a whole aims to reorient Christian imagination, both by portraying the limits of the common and persuasive mode of faith's engagement with culture that I define half playfully as "karma"–you get what you deserve–and by offering an understanding of grace as an alternative view. Grace–in which you do not get what you deserve–builds upon Scripture's portrayal of the very character of God, who responds to our cries. All the cries of human life, of creation itself, as David Ford puts it, are caught up into the "loud cry" from the cross, where God's participation in and transformation of our suffering is at its most profound. In this chapter, I invite you to consider what I called in the introduction "constricted imagination." In doing so, I'll portray the troubling internal logic and theological implications of an approach, rooted in the karma frame, that positions faith against culture.[5] To develop this view I'll introduce and discuss in some detail the influential evangelical organization Focus on the Family, and especially their entertainment ministry division, *Plugged In* (both a print magazine and a website). While they are an important and influential voice on these issues internationally–reason enough to choose them for the case study–they are simply one instance of a much more broadly assumed framework for relating faith and culture, especially in North America today. After some discussion of Focus and *Plugged In*, I'll use the karma–grace framework to make explicit the underlying theological framework their work assumes.

THAT GRIPPED MY HEART

The place to begin with Focus on the Family's ministry is in their basic impulse to help and heal the brokenness of the family. Jim Daly, currently president of Focus on the Family, articulates their basic organizational DNA in a video on their website's homepage titled, "The Focus Story." As Jim Daly comes into view, one sees the phrase, "In the beginning God created the family," on the screen. The Bible, he remarks, shows us that "the very first institution God creates is the family." The family is, in this portrayal, the basic building block of culture, and its shape is a healthy marriage between a man and a woman and their loving care for their children. What God set up in the very beginning, this foundation of culture, gives Focus their mission: "Helping Families Thrive." However, Daly is quick to point out, this mission is not easy to fulfill today.

As Daly describes his own family (two young kids, seven and nine), he voices concern about the culture his children are growing up in. While he speaks, this phrase appears on the screen: "The culture is not helping." Daly worries that children who watch TV with their parents in the evening "are exposed to so much that no child should have to be exposed to." The hope he expresses is a hope he imagines millions of parents across the political spectrum share. That hope is to have children thrive, to become good kids. It is hard to accomplish this task, Daly argues, because "we've got to do so much to protect our children today–the culture is not helping us to raise children." Focus steps into the gap, working to equip parents to help their kids thrive.

After a personal testimony about the importance of fathers who commit to their families, Daly turns to a concrete instance that creates an emotionally powerful end to the video. While the phrase "We can help" is shown, Daly describes hearing a recording of a 911 call from a seven-year-old who said, "My stepfather is about to hurt my mommy." That, Daly says softly, "gripped my heart." He wonders aloud how many more homes are not calling 911 when real tragedy is going on? This heart-wrenching scenario, not unlike the terrible incident with Tiffany Toribio, leads Daly to declare that we "need *more* Focus on the Families in this country to be able to stand there ready to provide help to those hurting families." To finish out the message, he thanks the many supporters who help Focus to "put an arm around a hurting marriage or a hurting parent who doesn't know how to deal with their teenage son who may be addicted to drugs. We can do better as a nation. We're standing in the gap, ready to help you with tools that can help your family thrive."

Focus on the Family, founded by Dr. James Dobson in the late 1970s, bases its operations on an eighty-one-acre campus in suburban Colorado Springs, Colorado. With roughly a thousand employees and an average of a quarter million inquiries a month (combined email, phone, and letters), it is clear that for many, Focus is the go-to source for help with family troubles of all sorts.[6] Dr. Dobson has bona fide credentials for this work with troubled families, having completed a PhD in psychology at the University of Southern California. He grew up in a longtime Nazarene family (his father, grandfather, and great-grandfather were all ministers) and belongs today to Eastborough Church of the Nazarene, in Colorado Springs. Nazarene theology emphasizes the free responsibility to choose faith in Christ's saving grace and afterward to live according to the rule of the Spirit, following a holiness code that includes no smoking, drinking, swearing, or other worldly pleasures.[7]

Such a religious background contributed to Dobson's very negative evaluation of the plight of families he saw during his decade as a professor of pediatrics at the USC School of Medicine. It was during this time, Dobson recalls, that his motivation to begin writing and speaking about family issues arose:

> My years at the USC School of Medicine and Children's Hospital, which came right on the heels of the sexual revolution, only

served to confirm my belief that the institution of the family was disintegrating. I worked with children on a daily basis, and saw firsthand how divorce, abuse and other forms of familial strife were tearing their lives apart. I became convinced that the only hope for these broken and disillusioned kids—as well as for future generations of children—lay in the strengthening of the family unit and returning to the Judeo-Christian concepts of morality and fidelity.[8]

He wrote his first book, *Dare to Discipline* (1970), to explicitly respond to the permissiveness of the 1960s.[9] Likewise, he began offering presentations and by 1976 had to take a leave of absence from USC. This effectively became his retirement from academic medicine. The radio show followed shortly after, partly as a way to stem the tide of invitations that were taking him on the road and away from home.

By 1985 Dobson was heard in a daily thirty-minute broadcast on nearly eight hundred radio stations nationwide. Mail poured in. In fact, the beginnings of Focus as an organization developed from the "correspondents" Dobson hired to reply to the letters, usually with advice from his many columns written for the radio show. From early on he also recognized the need to have a few therapists to counsel troubled and desperate people. When Focus relocated from Southern California to Colorado Springs in 1991, that part of Colorado had already become a mecca for evangelical Christianity. Home to NavPress, publisher of the bestselling *The Message* by Eugene Peterson, as well as such well-known organizations as Compassion International and the International Bible Society (now Biblica), this picturesque mountain community was a natural fit for the kind of work and workforce Dobson's ministry required. As the ministry expanded, the offerings both diversified and globalized so that by the mid-2000s Focus-produced radio programs were on more than five thousand stations in 155 countries, with an estimated global audience of 220 million listeners.

Even as global expansion has reached new heights, the age of the core constituency in the United States had risen to the high thirties, with the average age of persons on the mailing list reaching into the fifties. Clearly, Focus and its dependence on a nearly century-old technology was not catching the attention of a new generation. These younger potential constituents–not as likely to listen to the Christian radio that endeared Dobson to an older generation–began to see Dobson less as a family guru and more as a high-profile leader on conservative politics. Insiders worried about the image costs associated with occasional off-the-wall diatribes like Dobson's infamous attack on the hugely popular cartoon SpongeBob SquarePants as a supposed "pro-homosexual" character (an episode that closely connected him to Jerry Falwell, who similarly attacked the *Teletubbies* character Tinky Winky a decade before).[10] Even his more evenhanded forays into pop culture tended to be shrill, bent on proving that "wherever you choose to stick the thermometer, you can see that we are a nation in a great deal of trouble."[11]

SHINING A LIGHT

Focus developed a series of age-graded print magazines for children and teens throughout the 1990s. A key feature of this effort was the print magazine and now website on entertainment: *Plugged In*. Through its popular reviews of media–movies, music, television, videos, and games–*Plugged In* has grown dramatically in reach, especially since Jim Daly took over as president of Focus in 2005. With the goal of expanding the Focus audience to younger and broader evangelical and nonevangelical Christian demographics, Daly moved to Focus's first-ever network television ads and worked to use new avenues for distributing content. *Plugged In Online* gets roughly a million visitors monthly and creates weekly podcasts, one- or two-minute radio and television movie review shorts, and distributes an e-newsletter. These and other aggressive efforts show that Daly was positioning Focus to transition not only through Dobson's retirement (in 2009) but also into the new century, in which the thirty-minute radio show–if not dead yet–was becoming only one part of a sophisticated multimedia effort at Focus.

While Dobson has not served as a regular author of *Plugged In* content, his perspective sets the tone here, as it has throughout Focus as an organization. This is not surprising to insiders. Despite his folksy style on his radio show, Dobson is known inside Focus as "controlling," with a tendency toward "micromanagement."[12]

One can see Dobson's views on popular entertainment scattered throughout his books and many columns written in response to questions from constituents. Take, for instance, a column Dobson wrote in response to a listener who asked, "I remember adults complaining about the music of my day. Doesn't every generation of parents think their kids have gone too far?" Dobson took this question as an opportunity to review the popular rap album *Nasty as They Wanna Be* by the Florida group 2 Live Crew. The album is by all accounts nasty, and Dobson points out that it was banned as "obscene" by a Florida judge.[13]

More revealing, however, is the method Dobson follows in making his case for the problematic nature of this "music" (Dobson puts the term in quotation marks to accentuate his scorn). "At the risk of upsetting our readers," Dobson begins, "let me list for you–as discreetly as possible–the words that appear in the album *Nasty as They Wanna Be*. He begins with "226 uses of the f-word" and continues in systematic fashion, detailing all words that could be considered sex-related down to "one reference to incest." Noting that the album sold more than two million copies, Dobson warns that "youngsters–some only 8 to 10 years of age–buying this 'music' typically listened to it dozens, or perhaps hundreds, of times." While he roundly criticizes those liberal media figures who defended 2 Live Crew on either artistic or free speech grounds for failing to address the actual content of the lyrics, Dobson does not actually quote the lyrics either, nor does he speak with any youth who are fans. He moves from worries about youth listening to this album to make the point that "this is merely one salvo in an industry that has helped to destroy the moral code of Western civilization. It has accomplished this methodically and deliberately during the past thirty years, in cooperation with television and movie producers. The damage has been incalculable!"[14]

Plugged In has followed in Dobson's critical footsteps. Led by Bob Waliszewski, a twenty-year veteran at Focus, *Plugged In* is designed "to shine a light on the world of popular entertainment while giving families the essential tools they need to understand, navigate and impact the culture in which they live." *Plugged In* cites Colossians 2:8 as a biblical foundation for its work: "Watch out for people who try to dazzle you with big words and intellectual double-talk. They want to drag you off into endless arguments that never amount to anything. They spread their ideas through the empty traditions of human beings and the empty superstitions of spirit beings. But that's not the way of Christ." It highlights reviews of popular entertainment, acknowledging that while entertainment industry ratings offer some guidance for families, *Plugged In* "goes deeper, diving into specific content and the meaning behind it."

There is a remarkable similarity between Dr. Dobson's methods and those followed at *Plugged In*. Interviewing Adam Holz, senior associate editor, blogger Ted Slater asks why *Plugged In* reviews R-rated movies, especially when (as in the popular *Saw* horror movie series) the troubling content is pretty clear from the advertisements. Holz replied that of course there are good reasons not to review such movies, both because the content is rather obvious from advertising and because the films expose staff to exactly those things they ostensibly want their Christian audiences to avoid. But, Holz argued, evidence suggests that many people of faith are engaging in such entertainment, some without giving such choices much thought. "They're being shaped by the culture in deep and significant ways, and they're often not critically assessing the ideas, images, and worldviews that are washing over them."[15] In addition, many parents are seeking to make wise decisions with their children, who are more connected to media than ever before. Because youth are "swimming in a sea of non-stop images," *Plugged In* wants to help the parents, "the first and best line of defense."[16]

Having offered solid reasons for engaging questionable entertainment as part of the review process, Holz went on to describe that process. "The way we watch movies might be best compared to an autopsy," Holz explained. He described taking pages of notes during an average movie, making the experience "decidedly clinical." The aim in such clinical attention is to "look for positive messages and damaging worldviews, in addition to recording content concerns in the areas of sex, violence, drug use, language, and other negative content."[17]

This basic mode for reviews holds across most genres of entertainment (for example, Dobson's listing of the numbers of times each type of objectionable content appears in 2 Live Crew's lyrics). In a series of articles responding to Christian "metal" rock music, Holz adds a few additional points. First, the sound and imagery can be as worrisome as the words—as when metal bands combine violent imagery with biblical concepts. One typical outcome of this, Holz suggests, is that it "creates confusion." But in addition, the clarity of the words is important too. Holz quotes rocker Ryan Clark of Demon Hunter, who says that although they're "all Christians" in the band, he likes "to write in a more poetic and metaphorical style." Holz worries that the "penchant for penning obscure lyrics" leaves kids and families in the dark as to where the bands stand, spiritually speaking. I can't help but wonder what Holz would do with many of Jesus's parables, which his own disciples frequently found "obscure" but clearly were crafted with divinely inspired purpose (Matt. 11:15).[18]

JESUS WALKS

The hip-hop album from 2 Live Crew is a fairly easy target for anyone as worried as Dobson is about the moral decline of culture. Instead, let's look at another rap artist, Kanye West, whose Grammy Award–winning song "Jesus Walks" figured prominently in my presentation at Mount Vernon Nazarene University, recounted in chapter 1. West has certainly emerged as a controversial figure, exhibiting both astonishing musical and lyrical creativity and astonishingly self-centered bravado (an especially egregious example being his rude interruption of Taylor Swift during her acceptance of the 2009 Video Music Awards for Female Video of the Year). When his first album, *The College Dropout*, was released in 2004, he was known primarily as a producer based in Chicago with strong ties to New York hip-hop luminary Jay-Z, CEO of Roc-A-Fella Records. West quickly got the attention of critics with his combination of distinctive high-pitched samples from classic soul records alongside his unusual willingness to press the boundaries of lyrical content.

"Jesus Walks," the biggest hit from the album, received significant airplay despite his conviction–stated directly in the lyrics–that if he rapped about Jesus, the record wouldn't get played. In part, the narrator of the song is a struggling drug dealer who cries out to God but is unsure God will hear him, since "we ain't talked in so long." Yet the story of the song also shares the conviction, drawing on a powerful sample of "Walk with Me" by the ARC Gospel Choir, that Jesus walks with those who are crying out in despair, in the midst of addiction or prostitution.[19] "Jesus Walks" is, of course, only one song on the album, which I won't spend time engaging as a whole here (I return to West's work in the next chapter). It is more important here to show how *Plugged In* reviews such an album.

When *Plugged In* reviews an album, they categorize their response according to (1) pro-social content, (2) objectionable content, and (3) summary advisory. With West's *The College Dropout,* they duly note his shout-outs to God and Jesus as well as his critical comments about absentee fathers, materialism, and racism. Yet those three short sentences regarding pro-social content give way to a long and detailed paragraph under objectionable content. The list here follows the pattern Adam Holz noted as targets of his attention in reviewing movies: profanity, drugs, sex, violence, and other negative content. Between all the songs on the album, West pretty much hits every category of objectionable content, leading Holz to say in the wrap-up summary advisory: "West does his best to discredit education while exalting illegal, immoral behavior. Despite moments of social and spiritual conscience, *The College Dropout* should be expelled."[20]

CONSTRICTED IMAGINATION

In chapter 1, I introduced the term "constricted imagination" as a way to describe what *Plugged In* is doing when it "expels" *The College Dropout.* Here, I'd like to spell out a bit more carefully what theological understanding undergirds this perspective and how exactly it constricts Christian imagination. First of all, it is obvious that Focus and *Plugged In* have a default skepticism about the culture. The culture "is not helping," according to Jim Daly, Focus's president. Dobson argues that the culture and especially the media are "destroying the moral code of Western civilization." So it is no surprise that the motto of *Plugged In*, "Shining a light on popular entertainment," shares that skepticism.

On the one hand, this motto frames the challenge as one of investigation. Imagine the police searching a building for a criminal, shining flashlights from dark hallways into dark rooms. Such scenes cause our hearts to race and our worried imaginations to go into overdrive. On the other hand, shining a light introduces a doubt whether much, if any, light is already there in culture. The motto suggests that Focus and *Plugged In* have the light, and culture and its popular arts do not.

The skepticism about culture carries with it an assumption about how Christianity works out in practice–a kind of checklist Christianity. Whatever Dobson, Daly, or others at Focus might say if asked about their formal theological views, I'm interested here in the lived theology that they both practice and commend. Systematic theologians are not usually the first stop when the need is an understanding of practical Christianity, but the virtue their perspective offers us here is seeing the interrelatedness of claims about how God and the world work. Starting from the skeptical position in relation to culture, the Focus approach offers a "checklist" of concerns to measure whether particular media are acceptable or not. Presumably, people either adopt this same checklist in making their own judgments or simply take *Plugged In* at their word in judging some movie, game, or record as "safe" or "risky." At the heart of this process we find the goal is safety: our safety and the safety of our families.

The next chapter will more fully spell out why such checklist methods of discerning what "good" or "bad" cultural objects ought to contain gives way to constricted imagination. Here it might be enough to point out how kinds of knowing matter deeply, and the temptations of our age lean in the direction of "theories" and "explanations." C. S. Lewis articulated this in terms of the difference between *savoir* and *connaître*, two French verbs for "to know." *Savoir* indicates a kind of distanced and clinical "knowing about." The factual knowing, or *savoir*, Lewis implies, requires distrust of the object's own self-understanding and requires an over-against stance, a "looking at" something to make an independent judgment about it (presumably based upon some theory of what sort of thing it might be).[21]

One can easily recognize the clinical approach Focus and *Plugged In* take when reviewing movies, music, and so on. Lewis, rather, encourages engagement along the lines of the French *connaître* as a way to encourage looking "along" things or "with" them. The difference lies in knowing something experientially, from the inside, as it were. To know what pain means in a physiological or clinical sense without knowing the *experience* of pain is not in the end to fully know pain. In a gloss on this way of thinking, Paul Holmer wrote that with literature "one can have it spoiled by always viewing it through a literary theory and seldom if ever relishing the story and savoring the actual lines of poetry."[22] This approach admittedly is risky. But it is exactly in the risk to be fully engaged, fully human, that we are exposed to the sense in which the theoretical "knowing about" constricts imagination. While conscious that it was in some respects a more challenging way to live, Lewis was concerned "not to let a moral, poetical, or religious theory ever cut off the genuine discovery and drama of everyday life."[23]

KARMA AND GRACE

I titled this chapter "Karma and Grace." While I introduced the ideas at the outset of the chapter, here I can discuss in more depth what I mean by karma in relation to grace. Karma is a Hindu concept that has to do with actions that influence the future, and it is commonly invoked in theories of reincarnation. John Lennon's clever song "Instant Karma!" is funny partly because of its play on the idea that one's actions now will come around to influence the shape of one's next life.[24] "Instant karma" means you get what you deserve, but now instead of in the next life. Bono, U2's lead singer, has simply used karma as a way to speak about the basic pattern of getting what one deserves. If I do good things, then I expect good to happen to me; if I do bad things, then I expect bad to come my way. Whether now or later, actions have consequences, and those consequences are usually not all that surprising. The common phrase "what goes around, comes around" gets at how this idea plays out in everyday belief systems in the United States. In the complex history of India, such a belief system has served to keep a strict caste system in place by legitimating the dominance of some and the slavelike position of others.[25] In relation to Christianity, it picks up on a strain of belief and practice that emphasizes our decisions and their consequences. Such a framing of Christianity fits the characteristic way Focus and *Plugged In* speak of the life of faith.

Karma is an idealist perspective, because it wants to imagine that things *can* be as they *ought* to be. In this perspective, sin means primarily bad decisions and acts. People decide to swear, drink, take drugs, or make movies and records discussing these actions. The goal of Christian living is to avoid these actions or, in more classical terms, to avoid sin. While we are saved through the cross of Christ, the Holy Spirit works in our lives like a spiritual booster—a divine energy drink—that strengthens our ability to fight temptation.

Wesleyan understandings of grace lie in the background of Focus as part of its Nazarene heritage. While undoubtedly more nuanced in the theologically sophisticated works of Wesley and contemporary theologians working in this tradition, for practical purposes it ends up looking like the crass phrase "use it or lose it."[26] Once we've decided to give our life to Jesus and seek to live as his disciple, we are tentatively safe from the threat of death and damnation, but temptation lurks around every corner, and we must choose wisely in order to keep on the right side of the line between saint and sinner, between the church and a world lost in sin. In a nutshell, this framing of the Christian life reflects the aspects of karma we have been discussing. Certainty comes from my ability to act rightly, an ability I am empowered to use by God. If I do, I not only have heaven eternally but also live within the bounds of a holy community now, among the saints with whom I am safe, with whom I know I will be led according to right judgment in all things. The threat is, however, that if I do not choose purity and holiness in my actions, I fall from God's care and safekeeping into the darkness of a world that has lost its way. Such dire consequences result from stark framing of the issues and motivate the kind of rhetoric and action so prevalent with Focus and *Plugged In*.

THE TROUBLE WITH CHURCH-CULTURE DIVIDES

Focus on the Family and *Plugged In* share some basic concerns I want to applaud. Knowing God through the life, death, and resurrection of Jesus Christ would indeed focus our attention on the cry of the child whose home is broken by domestic violence, or the cry of the parent whose child has been caught up in addiction. Because such an impulse is so central to the animating core of Focus, and of Dr. Dobson's life and ministry, beginning with affirmation on that point seems essential. Dobson is, after all, a man who was trained and has worked his whole life in ministry with a goal of godly healing for individuals, families, and society. Over the years, Dobson has learned not to do radio shows on difficult issues like child sexual abuse too close together, because the flood of terribly difficult calls becomes overwhelming spiritually and emotionally for his staff of correspondents. He knows that lives are broken, and his God-inspired motivation has been to reach out with help.

The basic impulse to listen to the cries of suffering and brokenness in society and to respond shapes *Plugged In* as well. While this publication focuses particularly on an area of society (culture and entertainment media) that Dobson has singled out as very troublesome, it seeks to find within it examples of faith and the good life to encourage and support families. In an old tagline no longer used by *Plugged In*, it aims to offer a "Christian perspective on what to see at the box office, which TV shows are worth your time, and what music comes up clean." Anyone who has had a child of their own or has cared for children of another knows the basic impulse to protect the child from harm, and to reach out in an embrace once harm has been done. *Plugged In* does not intend to short-circuit family conversations about how to engage media but means to serve such conversations, to shine light on popular entertainment so as to illumine the conversations about faithfulness around tables in Christian homes.

Where does the Focus approach go astray, then? It is, as I've begun to show, the narrow vision of who God is and what ought to be considered legitimate material from and for a Christian imagination. A more robust theology of grace breaks apart the bounds of such constricted imagination about God and the world. It is true that strains of purity and holiness run back through Christianity and Judaism, exhibiting tensions between the sacred and the profane common to many religious traditions.[27] The polemical starkness of choosing between two ways seems endemic in Christian faith, and its history in the United States is particularly strong, given our Puritan founding as a "city on a hill" charged by the Reverend John Winthrop, echoing Deuteronomy 30, to "choose life."[28] Such arguments have a certain power, to be sure, but taken to be the decisive framing of life before God, they can lead, as they have done all too often in US history, to divides between a pure "us" and an evil "them."[29]

The term "constricted imagination" comes in when one asks about God in relation to such church–world divides. Imagining whole swaths of life abandoned by God, set "over against us" or, at the very least, "not helping" gives the distinct impression that God is small. Working from the assumption that the darkness of the world needs "our" light shone upon it might conjure up nice images of the Sunday school children singing "This little light of mine, I'm gonna let it shine." We should be chastened, however, by the conviction throughout Scripture that, as the psalmist puts it, "God made sky and soil, sea and all the fish in it" (Ps. 146:6).

In his lovely book of meditations on the church's creeds called *Tokens of Trust*, Rowan Williams likens the line "the almighty, maker of heaven and earth" to a person flicking a light switch. He argues that like the electrical current illuminating the room, God's creative power is constant and present, holding all things in their being, rather than in some way either present long ago or present only to that "sacred" portion of creation with whom God deigns to dwell.[30] Such a sensibility is surely close at hand when, in breaking open notions of love for neighbor to include "enemies and those who persecute you," Jesus said:

> When someone gives you a hard time, respond with the energies of prayer, for then you are working out of your true selves, your God-created selves. This is what God does. He gives his best–the sun to warm and the rain to nourish–to everyone, regardless: the good and bad, the nice and nasty. If all you do is love the lovable, do you expect a bonus? Anybody can do that. If you simply say hello to those who greet you, do you expect a medal? Any run-of-the-mill sinner does that. (Matt. 5:45–47)

From this and other similar passages the God we meet in Jesus Christ might be described as a prodigal God.[31] Jesus suggests that if we live lives formed by relationship with that sort of God, we too become prodigal: we give our best to all, regardless.

Like our prodigal God, so we are to be prodigal with the mercy and love we have received. We don't reserve our "rain" for the deserving any more than God does. If this is true, the challenge, as

C. S. Lewis helped us to see, lies in seeking relentlessly for those signs of God's presence and work under the surface of things. In his delightfully brusque manner, he says: "We may ignore, but we can nowhere evade, the presence of God. The world is crowded with Him. He walks everywhere *incognito*. And the *incognito* is not always hard to penetrate. The real labor is to remember, to attend. In fact, to come awake. Still more, to remain awake."[32] A world so full of God's presence and purpose as to be "crowded" with God hardly gives us the ability to set church against culture and to then take a step further to paint culture as "lost," "dark," or "against us." The absurd conclusion would be to say those same terms–"lost," "dark," or "against us"–are separate from God. Yet God in Christ experienced just those things in his abandonment on the cross. Exactly because of that reconciling abandonment on the cross we can be sure that God's reconciling work is in the midst of abandonment and darkness of all sorts, suffering with us and lovingly opening up possibilities for new creation.

If we say God rules only over the spiritual, calling us to engage only the pure and holy, then we're in danger of missing the point of God-in-flesh, Jesus. In fact, such a constricted view of God totters on the edge of a variety of early Christian views usually lumped under the label gnostic, which Christians have long set aside as heretical. One key aspect of such views declares matter evil, the idea being that our divine spark finds itself trapped in the material body. This very materiality, this fleshly body with its emotions and temptations, distracts us from seeing our true spiritual nature. Docetism was one key version of gnostic belief. *Docetism* is a term derived from the Greek *dokeō*, "to seem," and used to argue for an understanding of a Jesus who was actually pure spirit, not really physically human, one who suffered, died, and was buried, and on the third day was raised.

To allow for a less-than-fully-human Jesus is to not be deeply moved by his own compassion and the actions it inspired. Jesus, the Gospel writers tell us again and again, "had compassion" (*splanch-nizesthai*), a term that evokes literally "gut-wrenching" emotion (Matt. 14:14; Mark 1:41; Luke 7:13; and also Phil. 1:8). Again and again, Jesus was moved physically by the plight of the poor, the outcast, the stranger, and those made ritually impure by the letter of the law.[33] In his life, and particularly in his death, he moved with his own body as a bridge across those divides to reconcile and heal the chasm between humanity and God.

Focus on the Family rightly directs our attention to the very human cries caught up in the loud cry from the cross. This places God's reconciling self-sacrificial love at the heart of human life at its most abandoned, at its most broken. In this broken place, God is found reconciling the world to God's very life as God. God takes our suffering, our cries, into God's own life and opens the possibility of freedom beyond fear. So our freedom is not for our own safety in communities of the pure; rather, it is freedom to give away what we have in Christ in compassion for all those twisted and broken cries in popular culture. While you may now share some of my theological concerns about the constricted imagination one can see in the approach Focus on the Family embodies, that does not mean we give away our practical capacity for the kind of discernment about what is good and what is evil. No, that need remains, but the challenge looks different once it is clear that the line between good and evil, rather than running between the saints and the sinners, instead runs right through us all.[34] To the challenge for a new mode of discernment in and through a prodigal God-like surrender we now turn.

6

SURRENDER TO THE MUSIC

Is there anyplace I can go to avoid your Spirit?
to be out of your sight?
If I climb to the sky, you're there!
If I go underground, you're there!

—Psalm 139:7–8

INTRODUCTION

As I tried to show in the last chapter, Christianity's tendency toward constricted imagination stems from viewing pop culture as spiritually dangerous, as "guilty unless proven innocent." I learned this in high-school youth group when we were warned that playing rock records backward revealed demonic messages. This was famously charged to be true of Led Zeppelin's "Stairway to Heaven." Its positive-sounding title was given, we were told, so as to lure naive youth to the dark side. Adequately tempted by this warning, we tried our best to get the devil to speak to us, playing the song backward at various speeds, but we never heard more than a hilarious reverse version of lead singer Robert Plant's wailing. It was akin to when our teacher decided to humor us and played a classroom film backward (ah, what my kids miss now that everything has gone digital).

Just as with my experience with Led Zeppelin, many Christians do not heed the shrill danger warnings. They choose to engage mainstream pop culture rather than restricting themselves to the fruits of the multibillion-dollar industry dedicated to providing Christians with products guaranteed to be spiritually edifying. Adam Holz, the senior editor of *Plugged In* I introduced in the last chapter, argues as much. In defending *Plugged In*'s reasons for reviewing R-rated movies, he simply states: "The evidence suggests that many people of faith are consuming these entertainment products."[1] I have already described in some detail Holz's "autopsy" style of analysis, guided by a version of "checklist Christianity."

Interestingly, in the comments section after the interview with Holz, many readers posed ways of thinking about the issues much more akin to what I'd like to argue for in this chapter. Some responses predictably encouraged the approach of *Plugged In*. But a respondent named Tami suggested that with such an approach, "you're forced to look at it so critically and analytically, that you don't 'enjoy' it." She admits to having thought a lot about movies lately and asks rhetorically if "seeing this movie [will] make a positive difference in my life[.] Once those two hours are gone, they're gone. Will I be better, or worse, for the way I spent them?" Craig said, "I'm troubled though by the lack of distinction made between different sorts of 'R-rated' movies . . . many, many R-rated movies are serious and sometimes even great art." Another commenter suggests, "It's better to watch an R-rated truth than a G-rated lie. Movies like *Glory* are R-rated, but make me a better person."[2] Brenna, following up explicitly on Craig's comment, suggests "that the main thing required is discernment. . . . Just because a movie shows bad things doesn't mean that it is bad. . . . The best movies challenge, strengthen, and edify."[3]

Such reflective comments help connect back to the engagement I experienced with students, staff, and faculty at Mount Vernon Nazarene University (detailed in chapter 1) and open up the question of this chapter. What ought to guide our discernment? If the critical account I've given of "checklist Christianity" and the constricted imagination it forms is persuasive, then we need to stretch beyond such means of discernment. How do we make sense of more open-ended criteria rooted in the subjective question of whether I become a better person through my engagement with the popular arts? Here, I want to return to my engagement with C. S. Lewis toward the end of the last chapter.

Lewis's powerful vision helps to reorient our perspective from first of all judging whether the cultural object (song, movie, TV show) in front of us is good or bad (what he calls *savoir*, or knowing "about") and ask, rather, about what sort of people we become by attending to this or that cultural object (what he terms *connaître*, or knowing "with"). Lewis has, of course, been a very influential writer and thinker in Christian circles. Yet little serious engagement has been done to connect his overall theological position with his particular work of criticism of literature, particularly, or culture more broadly. Insofar as this engagement has happened, it has been surprisingly misleading. I offer one such prominent example of that below. My supposition is that if we know something of how Lewis understands God and the world, then we can make better sense of how he speaks of knowing whether some cultural object is good. We properly come to such judgment, Lewis argues, by attending deeply to it. The goal is to attend deeply enough to have some sense of how we might see the world through that perspective, or to say it differently, how an experience of that piece of art changes our humanity. That is, does it enlarge our being-before-God? To answer this question requires that we view pop culture as also the domain of God, as potentially spiritually edifying, and as "innocent until proven guilty."

DOING POPULAR CULTURE THEOLOGY

Framing the world as "innocent until proven guilty," however, can be misunderstood. Lewis shows up in a supporting role in many evangelically oriented writings on literature and the arts. Yet too often, as is the case with many great figures in the Christian tradition, Lewis is simply used as frosting on a cake the authors have already baked. Unfortunately, Fuller Theological Seminary professors Craig Detweiler and Barry Taylor have done just this in their engaging work *A Matrix of Meanings: Finding God in Pop Culture.* They have ostensibly drawn on C. S. Lewis as a foundation upon which to build their work.[4] Detweiler and Taylor begin *A Matrix of Meanings* with C. S. Lewis's famous quote on art and judgment.

> The first demand any work of art makes upon us is surrender. Look. Listen. Receive. Get yourself out of the way. (There is no good asking first whether the work before you deserves such a surrender, for until you have surrendered you cannot possibility find out.)[5]

This quote provides Detweiler and Taylor's starting place, underwriting their argument in the book. Yet they invoke it on their first page in an epigraph without any further analysis or explication. Doing so allows them to make of it something it is not.

As avid fans of pop culture, Detweiler and Taylor see a spiritual revival not so much in the church but in postmodern culture. Their aim, as they describe it, is "to create a theology out of popular culture rather than a theology for popular culture."[6] They argue that the makers of movies, television, music, and other cultural forms are already doing theology within popular culture. Detweiler and Taylor want to join them, thus relocating the center of contemporary theology from the academy and the church to the culture surrounding them. They evoke (but do not seriously discuss) the idea of "common grace" to defend their admonition to take a "closer look" at popular culture.[7] There, they claim, we can find the creative side of God, working in surprising ways and through unlikely voices. They see this pattern in Scripture, for example, in God's use of King Cyrus to restore the people of Israel from their exile, and God's speaking the truth through an ass to shame the prophet Balaam.[8] They claim the model of Jesus, who spent time in the streets engaging common people in the midst of their lives. On this scriptural basis, they argue for "reversing the hermeneutical flow," a technical phrase that means beginning not with theology or Scripture but with popular culture.[9] Such a method, they argue, helps them "rethink, reform, reinvent, and reimagine the gospel for the times in which we live."[10] They can propose such a bold agenda because they claim popular culture as a source of revelation: in the materials of popular culture they find "a lived theology that reveals the very nature of Christ and his kingdom."[11]

Barry Taylor's chapter on music offers a concrete example of how their aim to "rethink, reform, reinvent, and reimagine the gospel" works in practice. Taylor draws on more or less spiritually reflective musicians to elicit ideas he thinks the church ought to take seriously. One example is the British band Radiohead. Radiohead's bass player, Ed O'Brien, describes their humility as a band, admitting to never "getting it right." Taylor takes O'Brien's reflection and concludes that Christianity ought to worry less about orthodoxy, that is, about getting its truth claims lined up properly. I agree about the need to critique the "streak of perfectionism" that runs through American Christianity. But it seems specious to simply jump from O'Brien's offhanded remark to a critique of Christian perfectionism and its producing a "dearth of creativity in virtually every realm of the contemporary Christian experience, particularly the realms of theology and music."[12] Similarly drawing on a range of musicians, including Madonna and Nick Cave, Taylor finds a group of three "musical conclusions" to offer the church: embrace imagination and artistic creativity; address the "entire gamut of human emotions," including suffering; and last, to hold together body and soul, emotion and reason, sensuality and spirituality.[13] I don't have any argument with these conclusions per se; in fact, I like each of them. The problem seems to be justification: why are these admirable things to learn from pop musicians? Why these "lessons" and not others, such as George Strait's suggestion that if "all my ex's live in Texas," I ought to live in Tennessee? If we are stating that important theological claims are being made in pop culture, then are we not simply subject to the whim of our own taste, finding what we want to find in the songs we know? Why, in other words, should we trust theological insights from Ed O'Brien rather than George Strait?

The point here is that the strategy Detweiler and Taylor follow has serious methodological problems. On the one hand, such a method raises the question of how desirable a reimagined gospel might be were we to draw its substance from any number of shallow or twisted songs or movies. So the method of "allowing pop culture to speak for itself before we apply biblical interpretation" seems misguided, because it has not articulated a means of making judgments.[14] On the other hand, it is worth asking if one can (or should!) set aside one's presuppositions in order to let pop culture speak first.[15] When we listen to or look at anything, we draw on basic prereflective capacities–what Charles Taylor calls a "background"–to make sense of the thing at all. To make sense is to put it within a preliminary framework of meaning.[16] If we take seriously Taylor's description of the role of background in framing our knowing, then there is no way we can simply set all that aside and let pop culture set the agenda, not in any simplistic sense.

Try an experiment: see if you can set aside your own views and simply read these two hip-hop lyrics about guns.[17] In the second cut on 50 Cent's bestselling album *Curtis* (2007), titled "My Gun Go Off," he claims it is easy to "hurt you," rhyming a number of ways to say he'll kill you. He includes the promise that he's not "gonna stop hunting / Run run till you're spun." It's murder, he brags: "It's excellent execution when I'm pulling the trigger." From Kanye West's best-selling album *Graduation*, released the same day in a much-hyped competition with 50 Cent, here is a bit of the tenth track, "Everything I Am." He begins by claiming people wouldn't usually rap about people being shot and killed as a terrible thing, but in the last year alone, he claims, "Chicago had over 600 caskets." He critiques his hip-hop community: "killin's some wack shit / Oh, I forgot, 'cept for when niggas is rappin'," lamenting that someone might be killed for their jewelry or shoes. In despair or anger, he seeks out a pastor, in need of someone to talk to.

If you are like me, you'll not only have basic resources of language and sentence structure to make literal sense of the lyrics, but you'll also have interpretative frames that cause you to have gut reactions to the lyrics and the meaning you take from them. So we can't easily stop bringing our interpretative frameworks to pop culture. What about building a theology on the basis of pop culture? Can we build an adequate theology from "My Gun Go Off"? If we did, it would come out looking a lot like "an eye for an eye"–certainly biblical but not at the heart of the gospel (see Exod. 21:22–25, for example). "Everything I Am" offers something more–it could even be described as a prophetic critique of the centrality of violence in the intersection of urban and hip-hop culture. It appeals to the heart ("do you know what it feel like?")

and wonders if turning to the pastor, and by extension, to the church and God, might offer some solace.

But notice what I'm doing in each case. I'm engaging who I am and what I know in the interactive process of hearing and making sense with the grain of the lyric. I bring my sense of Christian values and the wisdom of theology and Scripture to my hearing, moving to meet the song's identity as I begin to understand it with my own identity in Christ. While I do not have a prescribed theory of what sorts of songs are "good" or "acceptable" (à la checklist Christianity), I do have basic cultural associations that allow the songs to have meaning for me.[18] It is in the act of seeking to understand, and then seeing "along" or "with" that understanding what it shows about the world, that I can make judgments. To explore such a process of discernment as a more promising way forward, I want to return to Detweiler and Taylor's starting point but then to go another way from that point. I agree that we must seek to set aside our first impulse of judgment. We need to, in a sense, set aside our looking "at" something. While we may look "at" these songs by 50 Cent and Kanye West and think, "That is rap music, which I _____ (fill in the blank: love, hate, etc.)," and make a decision on that basis, C. S. Lewis offers another way. He might put it this way: if hundreds of thousands of people are buying songs or seeing movies or watching a show on TV, it is worth asking what they are finding there that is meaningful, and how they are being shaped by their attention: how does such and such help them to see the world in a certain way?[19] Unpacking how such an approach works is our next step.

SEEING GOD WITH POP CULTURE

Like Detweiler and Taylor, I begin with Lewis's work in an attempt to build another way of connecting faith and popular culture. I too am struck by his claim that we must in some form "surrender" to a work of art if we are to understand whether it is any good. Yet by this Lewis does not offer a license to suspend judgment on works of art and to let them have their own say without our saying anything. Lewis's invocation of "surrender" as a first move in engaging works of art is more complex than that; or, perhaps better, it is more subtle and therefore also much more compelling. Lewis intended this admonition to surrender as part of a larger effort to reorient criticism of art from judgment about good or bad objects to good and bad use of the object, a shift that focuses on the person and not the song, movie, or painting. To understand more carefully what Lewis has in mind, both differentiating it from Detweiler and Taylor's use and making it available for us to use differently, I'll need to develop his meaning further through careful engagement with his little book *An Experiment in Criticism*.

Introducing Holmer's Lewis

First we need to step back and place *An Experiment in Criticism* in its broader context. I can only gesture at the outline of Lewis's life and work; yet, trying to place this one book briefly in context, especially as we come to grips with Lewis's mature thought, it becomes clear that his intellectual depth and seriousness have remained surprisingly hidden from view. While his many books on faith remain perennial bestsellers, the philosophical and theological coherence of his work is commonly overlooked. This is in part because of the very popularity and accessibility of his writing. My aim here, then, is to draw upon another subtle thinker and his outstanding book on Lewis that has stood the test of time: Paul L. Holmer and *C. S. Lewis: The Shape of his Faith and Thought*.[20] Through the lens of Holmer, it will be possible to elucidate the larger intellectual and spiritual framework with which Lewis worked in writing *Experiment*. We can thereby make clear how one might actually practice the sort of criticism of culture Lewis advocates.

Experiment was the product of a mature man, written near the end of his life, and in the sober aftermath of the death of his beloved wife, Joy. He had only met Joy Davidman a few years prior, but their short acquaintance and subsequent marriage had offered Lewis the happiest days of his life. An American writer, she had recently become Christian in part through reading Lewis's works and had begun a correspondence with him.[21] Travels to England, and finally moving there, allowed for the budding romance to develop. Just as their relationship took the turn toward marriage, her cancer reared its ugly head. The ups and downs of those few short years of their life together proved intensely trying. One can see the mark of it in *Letters to Malcolm: Chiefly on Prayer*, written around the same time as *Experiment*.

That *Letters to Malcolm*, the last book he completed, was less successful might have to do with the fact that it asks more questions than it answers. Lewis was willing to ask hard questions, questions that surely arose through the vicissitudes of Joy's illness. One example, which echoes the anguish he surely felt at Joy's suffering: "As for the last dereliction of all, 'My God, my God, why hast thou forsaken me?' How can we understand or endure it? Is it that God Himself cannot be Man unless God seems to vanish at His greatest need? And if so, why?"[22] A sobering and difficult question, one that surely connects with Lewis's own sense that God seemed to vanish in his and Joy's time of greatest need. Yet he struggles to speak to Malcolm of the life of heaven, of the pleasure found in all that is good in this life.

> How can you find any image of [the life of heaven] in the "serious" activities either of our natural or of our (present) spiritual life? Either in our precarious and heartbroken affections or in the Way which is always, in some degree, a *via crucis*? No, Malcolm. It is only in our "hours-off," only in our moments of permitted festivity, that we find an analogy.[23]

Such festivity is the exception in this life, he argues, yet Christians claim that everything is upside down in this life. What might be called utter irresponsibility in this life is an end in itself in that better country. "Joy," Lewis concludes, "is the serious business of heaven."[24]

The serious business of Lewis's life was a scholarly career in English literature, for many years at the University of Oxford and then in his last years in a new chair created with him in mind: Professor of Medieval and Renaissance English at the University of Cambridge. Throughout his career—from his 1936 work *The Allegory of Love* onward—Lewis challenged the dismissal of the late Middle Ages and its ways of thinking as merely outdated. He loved stories and, as a result of a rather sickly childhood, had a lot of time for reading, developing a deep affection for the wonder and imagination such stories evoke. Allegory, and story more generally, provides for Lewis a way to "show us something without quite arguing it. . . . Literature actually creates thoughts in us; it is not only about thoughts, it causes them to exist."[25] Key to this approach is Lewis's sense that literature ought not to be merely didactic, not a disguised theory, moral or otherwise; rather, it "creates new capabilities and capacities, powers and a kind of roominess in the human personality." His trust in such a mode is rooted in two beliefs: the possibility for growth, however difficult, in human beings and the rich diversity of the creation given to us by God. Humans, he might say, have the complexity and capacity to match the wonder of creation itself.

Lewis understands literature (or the arts generally) to work in such a way as to open people up. Pressing against the modern notion that general theories help us know and make judgments about what we are looking at, he suggests, through the voice of a character in one of his novels, that one cannot study human beings. That is, humans are not known by general laws; they are not "explainable." But there is such a thing as getting to know human beings. To know my cell structure or the chemistry of my brain or that my mother left me crying as a child are all useful bits of information, but they in the end cannot substitute for knowing me—my joys and sorrows, my experiences through life, and the relationships by which I navigate my daily routines. "Bulverism" is the term Lewis invents for the contemporary practice of dismissing something on the basis of a theory without ever actually engaging the thing itself to know if it might be true.

A classic moment from Lewis's famous novel *The Lion, The Witch and the Wardrobe* helps explain what he means by Bulverism. Two of the four children in the story, Susan and Peter, have gone to Professor Kirk's study, seeking his advice. Lucy, you see, has been to Narnia and returned breathless to tell of its magic, refusing to recant her claims. Following moral and psychological theories, they assume her to be either a pathological liar or mad, but the Professor suggests that they consider what they actually know of Lucy: has she always been a trustworthy sister? They admit so. Is she well in every other regard? Answer: yes. It follows, then, Professor Kirk says, that accusing her of lying or madness is not only very serious but quite illogical. If she is trustworthy, then they must consider the very real possibility that here, too, she is telling the truth.[26]

To understand the poet, the storyteller, the musician, or the artist, then, we must "begin by sharing the poet's words and consciousness, his way of seeing the world and people." By doing so we "see 'through' the poem; what we see is not the poet but whatever the poem happens to talk about."[27] In this way, we ultimately come to know God in and through coming to know the complexity of the world. This coming to know, suggests Lewis, means growing wise, gaining by experience the sorts of capacities of discernment and truth that help one to know that, after all, what can be seen through the poem is profound and of value. The norms for developing such wisdom require me to say more, but for the moment we can see that Lewis asks of us a more challenging path. Such a path, he argues, centers not on assent to dogmas but rather on living according to a way of life.[28]

It follows, then, that Lewis was deeply shaped by the moral perspective we call "virtues" as means of being habitually disposed. Contrary to the eighteenth-century philosopher Immanuel Kant, who championed universal norms and duties and distrusted the particulars of human life, impulse, emotion, and habit, Lewis thought the opposite. "For what you see and hear," he has a character in the *Chronicles of Narnia* say, "depends a good deal on where you are standing; it also depends on what sort of person you are."[29] Holmer describes Lewis as discovering something akin to what his contemporary at Cambridge, the philosopher Ludwig Wittgenstein, had argued, that there is a "grammar of thought and language which is not just one more permutation on theory making." The grammar, Wittgenstein thought, "would be known not by a theory but, rather, in the practical ways in which we put a sentence together. We simply do it; our linguistic behavior is ruled in practice without the rule being cited."[30] While Lewis did not apparently collaborate with Wittgenstein, he nonetheless came to a very similar standpoint. The good of human life, he thought, was far more about the "how" than the "what"; one can know "what" love is, but one spends a lifetime learning how to be a faithful and true lover. Here, we see the distinction I introduced earlier between knowing "about" things and knowing them experientially, as it were, through sharing feelings, thoughts, and points of view. I'll now turn to this distinction between knowing "about" things and knowing "with" them that is at the heart of Lewis's arguments in *Experiment*.

It might be surprising that in his grief over the loss of his wife, and in ill health himself, Lewis would rouse himself for a polemical intervention in literary criticism. Yet he had recently taken up his chair at Cambridge, where the atmosphere was strongly influenced by fellow English professor F. R. Leavis. Through his journal, *Scrutiny*, Leavis and his colleagues endeavored to rewrite the literary canon and create new standards for what stood as "good" literature. Not surprisingly, many of their choices markedly differed from those beloved by Lewis. He named this tribe the "literary Puritans," who, as biographer Alan Jacobs puts it, "wished to transform reading into an exercise in spiritual formation–an exercise guided by these strict Critics who would tell you what to read and why it was good for you."[31] They were, Lewis said, engaging in "criticism as a form of social and ethical hygiene. They see all clear thinking, all sense of reality, and all fineness of living, threatened on every side by propaganda, by advertisement, by film and television."[32]

Thinking of the previous chapter on Focus on the Family as a case study in what I've called constricted imagination, one could say the "literary Puritans" of Lewis's time have their contemporary relations, now in the form of cultural Puritans. Oddly, Alan Jacobs, who in many respects seems fair and thoughtful in his judgments about Lewis's life and literature, here suggests that *Experiment* "had nothing to do with Christianity."[33] Perhaps on the surface this is true, but as I hope to show now, its deep grammar is profoundly Christian and adheres closely to what Lewis himself calls elsewhere "the Way which is always a *via crucis*" (or "way of the cross").[34] That "scandal of particularity" encapsulated in the "loud cry" from the cross, a cry that makes space within itself for all the particular cries of history, gives theological form to Lewis's claims about surrender, attending, and seeking to share the place of those who cry out, seeking to see what might be seen, and to understand what might be understood, from that vantage point.[35] Yet that cry also has an answer, in the empty tomb on the third day; and in the very core of our faith, then, we find a proclamation that the cry is met by comfort, the despair met by hope, the sorrow of death met by a force of love that undoes death and offers, finally, a fullness of joy only glimpsed dimly in this life.

Learning from Lewis's Experiment

As C. S. Lewis embarks on his essay *An Experiment in Criticism*, he invites the reader to try out his proposal. Here we need to understand his proposal well enough to indeed try it out and thereby model for others how his critical approach offers a dramatic improvement over the "Puritan" variety he and I abhor. To begin, Lewis chooses a rather homely example. He observes that in his youth he loved Beatrix Potter's tales–*The Tale of Peter Rabbit*, for example. But as an adult, he realizes, he did not really attend to the illustrations as they were but rather used them as diving boards for his imagination. Their quality and actual detail did not much matter in his youth; however, as an adult he noticed the actual variability of quality in her drawings. He then moves to describe this as one of the main ways people approach art, including especially popular art. He writes, "You 'do things with it.' You don't lay yourself open to what it, by being in its totality precisely the thing it is, can do to you."[36] He is interested in whether the work of art can change us, and in order for the work to have a chance, we must "begin by laying aside as completely as we can all our own preconceptions, interests, and associations."[37] While he uses terms such as "surrender," or "have something done to us," he does not admit that the "right spectator is passive. His is also an imaginative activity; but an obedient one. He seems passive at first because he is making sure of his orders. If, when they have been fully grasped, he decides they are not worth obeying–in other words, that this is a bad picture–he turns away altogether."[38]

The key issue, then, is the question of how one arrives at the conclusion that "this is a bad picture," record, movie, television show, and so on. As Lewis takes his argument further, he draws upon music as an example. We first gravitate to the tune, he argues. We have a "social and organic response. We want to 'join in'; to sing, to hum, to beat time, to sway one's body rhythmically."[39] Then we have an emotional response, moving with the mood of the song into either a reflective or joyful or totally depressed place. The combination of melody and bodily responses sets us off into our imagination, and this, Lewis argues, is what most of us really enjoy. The songs take us to another place, so to speak. Such enjoyment qualifies in Lewis's terms as "use" of the song rather than actually attending to it for its own sake. If we merely love or hate the song, we may not have actually heard the song at all, or at best heard only the part that for our own set of reasons we happen to respond strongly to.

If we are to not make snap judgments about cultural objects, we must first actually attend to them in their own right and not simply accept or reject them based on our own sense of taste or values (in other words, based on whether on face value we can "use" them for our purposes); we must give ourselves over to it. Lewis wrote: "As the first demand of the picture is 'look,' the first demand of the music is 'listen.'" There may be a tune to hum or words to sing along with or recoil from, but "the question is not whether you particularly like that tune" or think the lyrics are nice. "Wait. Attend. See what [the composer] is going to make of it."[40] Don't be like the people who "rush forward to do things with the work of art instead of waiting for it to do something to them."[41] The great danger, Lewis writes, is that we "are so busy doing things with the work [of art] that we give it too little chance to work on us. Thus increasingly we meet only ourselves."[42]

Something terribly important is happening here, something deeply theological, yet the theological import of Lewis's meaning is not explicit. In juxtaposing these two responses to a song, we see a posture in one of waiting for the song to work on us and in the other of rushing to make the song into a tool that can work for us. In arguing for the first, a posture of waiting, Lewis presupposes and depends upon a conception of the role of sin as mediating between God and the world. Holmer helps sort this out by describing the notion of the self caught up in itself (or better, as the old Christian phrase would have it, "turned in upon oneself").[43] Such a person is trapped in a world of his or her own making and finds it hard to actually see—or listen to—others "standing right in front of me."

Strikingly, Holmer ties this to the modern predilection to separate experience and knowledge, as if one could experience something, ponder its meaning, and then find the appropriate perspective from which to make a judgment. In the opening paragraphs of his short essay on Bulverism, Lewis remarks on the troubles this predilection brings. He laments the "disastrous discovery" that we exist. That is, he writes, when instead of merely attending to a rose, we must think of ourselves looking, of the optic nerves and odor receptors, and by the end there is no rose left![44] Instead, Holmer argues, if one is set free from such a perspective, one can actually know something profound from the experience of simply seeing, hearing, truly attending.[45] Such freedom comes, one might say, in the freedom that comes from faith in a God whose judgment and mercy take us out of our selfishness and restore us to a community of self-giving and love. Faith in this understanding, then, does not rise or fall on rigid doctrine or moral rules but rather on freedom and restored relationships from which one takes "the long way," living within the Christian stories so that he or she knows "what it is to feel, to think, to judge, to hope, as a Christian."[46] Engaging this approach, Lewis argues, makes certain kinds of persons. They are persons who are growing, engaging, and through it all gaining proximity to the wideness and depth of God's goodness in and through the world's complexity.

Still, were we to attend to the world of popular music, we would find in its complexity things we would not wish to commend as "good." How do we become, and help others (I think of my now thirteen- and ten-year-old children) to become, the sorts of persons who are both open enough to bend their attention to the cries of the world but also able to make judgments that, in this particular case, the popular arts are indeed not good? I'd like to run an example in a more formal way now, to get practical and to see how this might lead us in a different direction than the Christian autopsy approach of *Plugged In* and others working out of a constricted imagination.

The first and most important shift Lewis accomplishes is on the first page of his book. Rather than viewing criticism as the process of judging good and bad books, he wants to ask about types of readers or types of reading. When *Plugged In* does its pop culture autopsy on Kanye West's album *The College Dropout*, it seeks to engage in a process of decision about the object: is it good or bad, safe or dangerous? Lewis argues such a habit of judgment "impedes reception." The habit of evaluation leads us to "fail of that inner silence, that emptying out of ourselves, by which we ought to make room for the total reception of the work." Young readers can guide us here: at "a first reading of a great work, they are 'knocked flat.' Criticize it? No, by God, but read it again."[47] Judgment is delayed, sometimes for a long time.

The way forward in making judgments comes through guidance in choosing stories, songs, films, and so on that do "knock us flat." It is a formation in association with the good that opens up the habits of being that allow us to know in fact what sort of thing this is in front of us. "A real and affectionate acquaintance with honest people gives a better protection against rogues than a habitual distrust of everyone."[48]

One cannot expect a young child to know how to make sense of a complex hip-hop album such as *The College Dropout*. The idea here is that capacity to engage grows in varied ways over time. Elements of formation that have helped my own children to see with Kanye West, to the extent that they listen to his music, stem partly from growing up in Atlanta and New Haven, having African American friends, teachers, and neighbors, and understanding important elements of American history (key among them the legacy of slavery and the fight for freedom and dignity). They have also had a lifelong formation in the stories of Jesus, thinking through with their parents how his deep compassion for those who were lost and hurting gives shape to the posture of our own actions as a family. This formation has prepared them to hear a song like "Jesus Walks" and make sense of its juxtaposition of drug dealing, urban poverty, and Jesus in the midst of it all.

There are other important themes in the album, for instance, the irony and social criticism in its title and ongoing themes about how education does not pay off in the ways American culture promises (something like: work hard, stay in school, and you'll be successful). The album also deals with how drug dealing "just to get by" plays a dominant role in many young African American lives. Certainly some of these themes require greater sophistication to make sense of than we might reasonably expect of a child.

Engaging in a discussion of the religious and cultural sophistication necessary to really listen to a hip-hop album leads us to Lewis's second key point. Following the direction of his "experiment" leads us away from the category of "taste" as central for judgment. If I say Kanye West is a hip-hop prophet, and you say he is a profane egomaniac, we are at loggerheads, each operating with our independent categories of taste and judgment. But if we attend to what sorts of people we are as a result of an encounter with West, and how we describe the nature of our opinions in relation to what

West has actually done, soon we would find out the depth of our attention to the artist and his work. Lewis is instructive here, and transposing his example slightly from his imaginary author Mr. Lamb to our hip-hop example Mr. West, we can see the shallowness of judgment based on taste.

> Suppose you had given me enough rope and let me hang myself. You might have encouraged me to talk about Lamb, discovered that I was ignoring some things he really has and reading into him a good many that aren't there, that I seldom in fact read what I so praised, and that the very terms in which I praised it revealed how completely it was for me a mere stimulant to wistful-whimsical reveries of my own.[49]

The idea here is judgment—positive or negative—that results from projection of ourselves onto the book or song, and leads to the actual thing itself being rejected without ever being understood. As Holmer says, interpreting Lewis here, it is not simply knowing facts (the f-bomb is dropped forty-two times) or having a theory of pop music at hand, but it is a relational act such that through an encounter persons come to know in the sense, as Holmer writes, that presupposes "a readiness to see, a facility to size things up, a quickness to understand."[50] Such knowing comes from living a life, and the discerning engagement with culture aids this growth.

So, Lewis continues, if making judgments merely on the basis of taste leads to critical judgments without understanding, then his proposal makes criticism harder. "Nothing," Lewis writes, "is less illuminating than to read some author who is presently under a cloud (Shelley, say, or Chesterton) for the purpose of confirming the bad opinion we already had of him."[51] Here, the formation is in blind taste, in a theory of what makes good or bad literature, films or songs. Is there profanity? Reference to drugs? Violence? Sexuality? Check. Then, according to the cultural Puritans, it must be unworthy. Lewis turns from this stance, seeking to convince us that "adverse judgments are always the most hazardous," partly because of his strong sense of the difficulty in really understanding another person.[52] "A true knower," Holmer writes, "has to equip himself or herself, transform and sensitize abilities so that words . . . will become something like spectacles to look through, not look at."[53] Instead of evaluative critics, Lewis suggested, he'd rather have as his friends "editors, textual critics, commentators, and lexicographers" who could help him "find out what the author actually wrote and what the hard words meant and what the allusions were to."[54] The acid of the critical eye, it turns out, burns those upon whom it lands. "You cannot be armed to the teeth and surrendered at the same moment."[55]

In the surrender, the difficult act of seeking to understand another takes center stage. Curiosity and generosity become partners in the quest to know what one can see *with* the artist's point of view. In seeing with another's point of view, the question can be asked how people appropriate the art, and who they become as a result. Listening to the song "Jesus Walks," and reading many commentators (including much fan commentary online), leads me to conclude that it embodies the very reasons the album *The College Dropout* as a whole is good. As my kids and I listen to the song, and watch the Chris Milk–directed video for the song, a couple of key things happen.[56] First, complex issues of race and class are front and center. As a privileged family–Caucasian, educated, solidly middle-class with a nice home in the neighborhood next to Luther Seminary–we find ourselves with new proximity to social problems through the challenging questions West raises about living in poverty or struggling against racism in the workplace or educational system.[57] Second, the song's later lyrics take on the music industry and media, generally claiming you can sing about "guns, sex, lies, video tapes," but if you rap, as he does, about God, then the record will not be played. Yet his deepest desire is to hear, the next time he's in the club, "everybody screaming out Jesus Walks." Here we see a compelling complexity: the paradox of criticizing the very industry in which you seek to find success.

Last, the song's core theme of Jesus walking with those who are down-and-out draws our eyes to the heart of the gospel, that while we were yet sinners Jesus died for us (Rom. 5). It goes against the common idea that one must be holy to be in proximity to God and that we can actually be holy enough to deserve that proximity on our own. Che Smith, a Chicago-based friend of West's who raps under the name Rhymefest, got "Jesus Walks" started and shares half the song's royalties, but he thinks the song is "all Kanye." Smith comments,

When he wrote, "To the hustlers, killers, murderers, drug deal-
ers / Even the strippers / Jesus walks for them!", I said, "Wait, it
doesn't matter what you do at all? You can keep doing bad things,
and in the end it's all good? Don't we need to take a stand?" And
he said, "It's about imperfection. Everybody can relate to that."
Damn if he wasn't right.[58]

The very fact that the beautiful sample behind West's rapping on
"Jesus Walks"—taken from the ARC Gospel Choir's song "Walk
with Me"—is sung by a choir of those recovering from addictions
helps make the case. The imperfections are there, both in the songs
and in the life West lives. It's exactly because of the complexity, truthfulness, and beauty of his music that West ought not be
expelled, as the *Plugged In* review suggests. Rather, with Lewis,
I might say that if even one person has really listened and taken
Kanye's hip-hop art to heart and has become something more as
a person and as a Christian (and I have), then we cannot so simply
dismiss his work as beyond the pale. Some may indeed believe that
Kanye and all hip-hop are bad, but in taking C. S. Lewis's experiment seriously, one can find that it is bad only by listening to it
"as if it might, after all, be very good. We must empty our minds
and lay ourselves open."[59]

Surrender and the *Via Crucis*

In concluding this chapter I'll pull some threads together that
make explicit Lewis's call to take on the logic of the *via crucis*
and live its grammar in the daily encounters of our lives. In the
epilogue of *Experiment in Criticism*, Lewis finally makes explicit
the theological grounding that has been present throughout this
little book, giving cosmic sense to the basic argument, a theological
justification for his experimental method of cultural criticism.
Because we are finally sinful, self-centered people, the "primary
impulse of each is to maintain and aggrandize himself."[60] This is,
as I said earlier, a gesture to the profound effect of sin as a pervasive fault that twists our whole being "in upon itself." We become
supremely narcissistic, even imagining our actions to influence
God positively or negatively.[61] Lewis imagines that the result is
that we become "Leibnitzian monads" whose main characteristics

are being individual, subject to our own laws, uninteracting, each of us reflecting the entirety of reality within ourselves. Such an idea connects with the modern myth of the autonomous rational individual, a key element of both contemporary political and economic ideologies.

Rather, Lewis speaks of the role of Logos (one hears here the biblical idea of Jesus as the preexistent Word that became flesh–see John 1:1) that offers, through material creation–arts, literature, music, and so on–"a series of windows, even of doors." "One of the things we feel after reading a great work is," Lewis writes, " 'I have got out.' Or from another point of view, 'I have got in.' "[62] Here, Lewis presses against the self-focused pattern of seeking only to fulfill my own desires and suggests we also might follow a "secondary impulse," which

> is to go out of the self, to correct its provincialism and heal its loneliness. In love, in virtue, in the pursuit of knowledge and in the reception of the arts, we are doing this. Obviously this process can be described either as an enlargement or as a temporary annihilation of the self. But that is an old paradox: "he that loseth his life shall save it."[63]

Lewis quotes Mark 8:35: "Whoever finds his life will lose it, and whoever loses his life for my sake will find it" (NIV). It is a paradox at the heart of Christian life. Once transformed toward the neighbor rather than literally being stuck on ourselves, we "delight" to enter others' beliefs, passions, and imagination, even when we feel they are untrue, depraved, or lacking all realism. Lewis makes clear that this is not for the sake of gratifying some voyeuristic curiosity about the other–their psychology or history or moral convictions. Nor is it to perform some critical "autopsy" on them in order to come to a shortcut to judgment about their worth. It is not that kind of knowing (again, what Lewis calls *savoir*) at all. It is knowing (*connaître*) "in order to see what they see, to occupy, for a while, their seat in the great theatre."[64] One senses here that his larger aim is both dislocation of the self and at the same time healing, seeking exactly through the dislocation a wholeness that comes from being made one with God in Christ, and thereby awakening to a world "crowded" with the presence of God.

Lewis points to the paradoxical center of Christian faith in simultaneous disruption and healing of the self. A true theology of grace must lie here, and the great saints have known this. As Rowan Williams wrote in *The Wound of Knowledge*, their greatness lies exactly in their "readiness to be questioned, judged, stripped naked and left speechless by that which lies at the center of their faith." This is true, Williams argues, because

> the final control and measure and irritant in Christian speech remains the cross: the execution of Jesus of Nazareth. Christianity is born out of struggle because it is born from men and women faced with the paradox of God's purpose made flesh in a dead and condemned man.[65]

Indeed, the Mark passage just prior to the one Lewis quotes is this:

> Calling the crowd to join his disciples, he said, "Anyone who intends to come with me has to let me lead. You're not in the driver's seat; I am. Don't run from suffering; embrace it. Follow me and I'll show you how. Self-help is no help at all. Self-sacrifice is the way, my way, to saving yourself, your true self. (8:34)

The fact of the cross, and the response to the cross, God's raising Jesus on the third day, creates the ground upon which our own reconciliation stands and from which mission is set loose in the world. God's paradoxical action sets loose this force of love and mercy, and the disturbing implication is, Lewis might agree, "that God provokes crisis and division."[66]

The perspective I lightheartedly call karma imagines that we can, with a divine boost, do what is required to be pleasing to God. We can follow the "law" as Paul puts it. Yet Paul's exact point is that the law is responsible for the death of Jesus. The theology of the cross, as I have described it in the introduction, "calls a thing what it is." Our optimistic dependence on our own ability to keep the law and to make a deal with God in our favor leads to false certitude about our saintliness and the sin of the world. As Rowan Williams puts it, "God provokes a crisis to destroy our self-deceiving reliance on 'Law'; our dependence on what we as individuals can make and sustain, or what we as societies can administer for our own unchallenged interest."[67] The cross calls us what we are, naming our sin as fatal, disrupting our capacity to make up the life we think we deserve, so that drowned in the "chaotic waters of Christ's death, . . . the Spirit can move to make a 'new creation.' Being unmade to be remade."[68]

Indeed, then, a theology of grace views all as broken, and God's work through the cross as reaching into every space of abandonment and brokenness, responding to every cry, with a mercy and love that reaches deeper than the despair, pain, and sorrow. So it is that we must lose our life in order to find it. Our very pride and sense of deserving righteousness must be stripped away in order to find ourselves born again in the image and likeness of God (Gen. 1). To think this healing can happen short of such deep hurt is folly. Here, Paul's brief comment gets it right: "I deliberately kept it plain and simple: first Jesus and who he is; then Jesus and what he did—Jesus crucified" (1 Cor. 2:2), meaning that it is an illusion that God is to be found apart from Jesus crucified. In our "self-annihilation," as Lewis puts it, space is opened up in us for God and neighbor; we are opened to others, we find within us the compassion (*splanchnizesthai*) to really see, to hear, to understand. God "gave over" Jesus to be rejected by the world. This giving over made space within God's own life for the fullness of human life so that God could disrupt the violence of the law with love. Only through such a divine move could we be disrupted by the cross and find ourselves born anew into the expansive embrace of God's mercy. It makes sense, then, that, as Rowan Williams puts it, "the most clear and enduring mark of Christian identity is . . . an entirely costly *disponsibilité*, availability in service which gives no room to the superficial interests of the ego."[69]

This we share with all people, indeed all creation. Broken, we cry out and find ourselves addressed by the disruptive love of the crucified God, who in merciful patience is reconciling the world.[70] Our living into such mercy grows; it is neither fully completed nor static as we move day by day. Paul speaks of putting away childish things, a kind of growth in maturity in Christ (1 Cor. 13:11). Martin Luther spoke of yeast working in the loaf; the yeast is at work even if the loaf is not fully leavened.[71] C. S. Lewis, rather, thought of our gaining a kind of wisdom through compassionate understanding of the other. Our lives are lived for others. How better to have our lives formed according to the pattern of Jesus's own life than to give ourselves over to actually knowing well and fully those to whom we are called in loving service.

Lewis concludes the book with this comment about the perspective granted through seeing with or through the arts–a poem, a book, a song: "Here, as in worship, in love, in moral action and in knowing, I transcend myself; and am never more myself than when I do."[72] This theology is rooted in his understanding of the cross and the shape of self-giving life that comes through the reconciliation known through that cross. One might describe it as a "carnal" theology. It is a physical, bodily theology. It follows the shape of our Lord's actions in opening himself again and again to those on the margins: women, tax collectors, the sick, children, Gentiles. Christ was the Word who became flesh (John 1), the one who while being one with God took on our human form, humbling himself for our sake (Phil. 2). Christ comes to us again and again in sacramental form, broken open for us at the center of the assembly of believers through word, water, bread, and wine. By being joined to his death and resurrection through baptism, our lives share this shape, this bodily self-giving for the sake of a world in great need.

Yet too often Christians seek with all their might to hold on to their life in Christ. They run from "secular" culture, reject the popular arts in all their beauty and terror, and seek the purity and safety of their own Christian ghetto. As we have found through trying on C. S. Lewis's "experiment" in engaging pop culture, such a fearful response fails to fully answer our Lord's call to follow. In trusting that Christ's mercy is sufficient, we are enabled to give ourselves away to a broken and hurting world, seeking to understand it, love it, and ultimately share in its midst God's ongoing work of reconciliation.

7

PRACTICING SURRENDER

Doing something for you, bringing something to you—
    that's not what you're after.
Being religious, acting pious—
    that's not what you're asking for.
You've opened my ears
    so I can listen.

                          —Psalm 40:6

In *At The Crossroads*, his powerful critique of contemporary Christian music (CCM), artist and producer Charlie Peacock describes the rise and fortunes of Christian pop music from the perspective of an industry insider. Echoing his title, he describes that industry as being "at a crossroads." Interestingly, he evokes the legacy of Robert Johnson, who supposedly traded his soul to the devil at the crossroads and sang about it in his 1936 recording, "Cross Road Blues." Peacock then suggests Jesus was at the crossroads in Matthew 4. He faced the devil in the desert, but instead of trading his soul for fame and power in this life, Jesus rejected the devil for the sake of the kingdom. This is the perpetual challenge, Peacock argues: to choose "between the kingdoms of this world and the kingdom of God."[1] When making discerning choices about pop culture, insiders to this Christian music world often simply say, "If there's no Christ, it's not Christian."[2] *Broken Hallelujahs* is an attempt to show how posing the question this way, despite its seeming obviousness for many Christians, leads us astray in our efforts to live with a vibrant and deep Christian imagination in the world today.

If you have come alongside me through the first six chapters, then such a simple "no Christ, not Christian" approach or its opposite, "yes culture, yes sin and the devil," ought to raise your eyebrows. Yet, as Andy Crouch shows in his masterful and important book *Culture Making*, versions of this approach are part and parcel of the trajectory of evangelical Protestant Christian responses to culture.[3] He describes the rise of fundamentalism around the turn of the twentieth century as a reaction to Darwinism and the historical-critical method in biblical studies. Subsequent loss of cultural influence led to a stance of condemning culture, which is portrayed as something separate and dangerous, something we ought to withdraw from into "kingdom living." While this perspective still remains powerful (influencing Focus on the Family, for example, and even the various mainstream rating systems for movies, music, and games), Crouch shows how other stances arose through the twentieth century. Francis Schaeffer and others argued for cultural engagement and critique, while John Wimber and other founders of contemporary Christian music copied culture, asking, "Why should the devil have all the good music?" Today, Crouch argues that these patterns of response to culture–condemning, critiquing, and copying–have given way to simply consuming culture.[4]

Crouch would have smiled knowingly had he been with me at Mount Vernon Nazarene University and heard the students playing Kanye West in the media booth at the back of the lecture hall. He suggests that culture is not some distinct area from which we can remove ourselves. The impulse to withdraw from culture actually blinds us to how it is the very water we swim in. Rather than continue to recommend some version of withdrawal and critique of culture as a means to its transformation, his book offers a biblically grounded and sociologically sophisticated call for Christians to join in making culture as a way to change the culture. To those worried about culture, he might say: what we need is not more "Christian" art but rather more Christians making art. In doing so, the Christian tribe can witness to God through its arts as part of a cultural conversation God's already in on. This is a powerful argument, one I appreciate and encourage. Yet this book takes a different tack.

Rather than placing the weight on the Christian "tribe" whose task it is to "create" culture, this book calls us to discern the cries–Christian or not–trusting that God is present in the midst of them. As the psalmist says at the top of this chapter, God isn't after us to do something for God–especially walking about declaring how "religious" we are. Rather, God has opened our ears so that we can listen to what God is listening to–bending an ear near to the cries of love and loss, sorrow and suffering, and moving in the midst of them to witness and join God's work of new creation (2 Cor. 5).

I'll briefly take stock of where the argument of the book has come to before concluding with three examples of the practice of surrender I mean to encourage. The first part of the book explored the theological and biblical theme of brokenness, cries of suffering and sorrow, and how the Scriptures tell us God is especially present there. The second part of the book described an influential Christian approach to pop culture I've called "checklist Christianity" and an alternative that takes its pattern not from a moral code but from a crucified and risen Lord, Jesus. His very life—taken, blessed, broken, and given for the sake of the world—offers us a pattern as we engage the world and its wild cacophony of pop-culture creations.

The pattern, as described by C. S. Lewis, requires giving ourselves away to the other, fully expecting to meet what God is doing in and through them. It may indeed be that the creative power of God is so twisted (say, in the *Saw* movies released every October over the past few years) that all one can see there is brokenness.[5] Yet even there, this perspective might say, we can see the creative power of God. For Jesus teaches, "This is what God does. He gives his best–the sun to warm and the rain to nourish–to everyone, regardless: the good and bad, the nice and nasty" (Matt. 5:45). Here, Jesus is teaching about loving enemies. What good is it if we love only those who are "good Christians," as my grandma used to say? When she said that, she acted as if such a judgment was the litmus test for whether we ought to listen to what someone had to say. I want to argue, to the contrary, that even if something in pop culture is so twisted that its portrayal of horror only offers a broken cry, that cry is worth hearing. Why? Because Christ is in that cry, God listens to that cry, and we Christians *as* the body of Christ ought to hear it too. The *Saw* films may not, in the end, be any good. They may not be redemptive in any way. Our family would never take our kids to see them, and I wouldn't ever want to see them myself (as it turns out, I dislike the horror genre in general). It is worth saying, furthermore, that those who produce the films and those who see them likely don't understand what they are making or consuming in this theological perspective. Yet, if the theological framework I have developed thus far holds water, such cultural creations *cannot* be Godforsaken. More than that, we can't *know* whether *Saw VII* or Kanye West's album *My Beautiful Dark Twisted Fantasy* or any other cultural production is any good unless, following C. S. Lewis's understanding of Christian discipleship, we have practiced surrender.

An obvious shorthand for this invitation to practice surrender is C. S. Lewis's simple (but *not* simplistic) juxtaposition of looking "at" something with looking "with" it. Looking "with" something is, he agrees, not the easier of the two ways. We don't have time enough for surrender to each cultural creation, and so we cannot always know whether what we see when looking "with" it is any good, for us or for the world as God intends it. That is why, after all, constricted imagination is such a common approach to pop culture. The constriction leads to a checklist that can be certain, clear, and easy. Accept this, reject that. Yes! Done! I am sympathetic to the ease of this approach. I too want a way to make judgments about the music, film, games, and other popular arts I engage. Yet, if this book has done anything, I hope it has raised serious theological doubts about such an approach. God gets terribly small when we follow the trail of constricted imagination: God's here (with me), God's not there (with you). No, I say! Just when we think we have got that one straight, Jesus gives us the parable of the Pharisee and the tax collector, and the sinner comes out looking the better (Luke 18:9–14).

Dan Kimball, in his book *Emerging Worship*, inadvertently portrays an example of how checklist Christianity leads into a "small god" trap. He admits to loving the Ramones, a band that bucked the disco trend in the 1970s and came crashing onto the New York music scene with a powerful stripped-down version of rock and roll that would come to be known as the punk revolution. Kimball clearly loves their music, and even more their pioneering spirit, going against convention to create a new musical path. He notes that Bono, in presenting an award to the Ramones decades later, credited them with inspiring U2's birth. Yet, quick to anticipate critics of using the Ramones as a role model, he writes that they "were a rather pagan band that by no means held to Christian ethics or morals. I am not endorsing their personal lifestyles or saying God was behind the birth of their music."[6] But I want to argue that God is not the God only of "good Christian" singers. Indeed, God *was* behind the birth of their music, even through the many ways their lives and music lifted up a profound experience of the brokenness of life. But such a complex understanding of the Ramones requires the kind of approach I'm calling the practice of surrender.

What, then, does the practice of surrender look like in use, so to speak? How does one go about it? I've given examples along the way, seeking to practice surrender with Leonard Cohen's folk ballads, the blues of Billie Holiday, Ma Rainey, and Thomas Dorsey, as well as Kanye West's hip-hop. The cultural Puritans of checklist Christianity would reject any of these. To quote one example, a reviewer at *Plugged In* dismissed Leonard Cohen's song "Hallelujah" as offering only "muddled biblical references" and fixation on "the bleakness of love gone cold."[7] Such an evaluation of what many consider the greatest pop song of all time emerges from looking "at" it.[8] I have tried to show how we can reach a different conclusion through the untimely practice of surrender, which allows looking "with" the song, and with Cohen himself.

Now to conclude, I'll offer what I hope you'll consider benedictions: good words to be sent out with as you practice surrender in your own engagement with popular culture. I'll start with the Harry Potter book/film series. Then I'll engage with two groups I've grown to love over the past few years. The first was introduced to me by a student of mine: the postrock Icelandic band Sigur Rós.

The second, Arcade Fire, I first heard via U2–they are regularly cited by U2 drummer Larry Mullen as his favorite band (after his own, presumably).[9] I could engage so many examples I know and love, both from the United States and abroad. Tinariwen's African blues-rock rooted in the political struggles of the nomadic Tuareg peoples of the Saharan desert region of North Africa would offer a fantastic case study.[10] So would Junoon, the Sufi rock band from Pakistan whose lead singer, Salman Ahmad, is often called the "Bono" of the Muslim world for his activist work.[11] I hope that among other things this book can inspire an imagination in Christians to engage the immense creativity in the wide world of pop music and pop culture today. While these additional case studies are few and intentionally abbreviated, they do offer some indication how this can be done, and then you, dear reader, can take it from there.

HARRY POTTER

As have many families around the world, my family read J. K. Rowling's Harry Potter series. We had not, however, gone to see any of the movies. The final movie (broken in two parts released in winter 2010 and summer 2011) finally won us over, and in preparation for its release, we began to watch the movies together. Our son, now thirteen, finished reading the series years ago and reread them all in preparation for the release of book seven on the silver screen. Our daughter, just ten, finally read the last two volumes in the series. When the series first came to our attention, we had to ask the question about reading the books at all, and now we're asking questions about watching the films.

One of the obvious questions raised by checklist Christianity has to do with the basic plot of the series: the existence of a parallel magical world into which Harry Potter is thrust on his eleventh birthday, when he receives his letter of acceptance to Hogwarts School of Witchcraft and Wizardry. A simple search for "Harry Potter" and "Satan" on Google turns up literally thousands of sites purporting to show how the series makes evil look innocent and leads unsuspecting children to witchcraft.[12] As the series continued, typical issues arose alongside the complaint about witchcraft—violence, of course, but also the typical checklist worries: profanity, drinking, and sex. These are worth worrying about, and I don't want to deny that. It is partly the terrible violence that keeps me from horror movies as a genre, despite my own claim that I can't know that they are horrible simply because of that fact. Yet, if such a checklist leads us to reject the Harry Potter series simply by looking "at" the series, then we are in danger not only of rejecting God's work but also, as C. S. Lewis puts it, of rejecting a work that might "after all be very good."[13]

As I argue in chapter 6, a key issue for the practice of surrender is training in discernment and formation of character in community. The closest example to what I'm after is modeled by Calvin College's Ken Heffner, director of student services and champion of engaging pop culture as part of growing in Christ. As I have worked these questions myself, friends have said to me, "Chris, you should meet Ken." I think, rather than repeating again what I think this approach is about, I will try to describe something of Heffner's efforts at Calvin. First, Heffner depends on a community of Christian faith formation. "The theological ideas and Christian discernment they are learning in classroom" builds upon their childhood formation in home and church. But without using this knowledge, Heffner argues, such knowledge is of little use. "The ideas kind of die on the vine if they don't get practiced." So, both through a campus concert series and through the bienniel Calvin Festival of Faith and Music, Heffner flips what typical colleges do with student services. Rather than simply provide an escape from classes with a live concert series, Heffner creates a sort of laboratory where the students can engage popular culture, experiencing the work of popular artists in the context of forums, online blogs, and live interviews with the performers. Such lively conversation creates both the context for receiving the gift of the performer's music and a context in which to ask the deeper questions that lead to "seeing with" that performer in such a way as to know how and why it is good, and where it might be bad, or at least worrisome.[14]

Such an experiential learning process in community fits the sort of process I think C. S. Lewis means when he speaks of "surrender." It is not, I've said before, making oneself a blank slate; that is not even possible. It *is* my reserving judgment long enough to let the work of art speak to me, trusting on the basis of a robust theological vision that I ought to do this self-emptying to meet how God is at work in the midst of the world. And it is key that I do this in conversation, formed by life in community—be it home, church, or, as in the Calvin case, a college. Heffner grounds his work in a vibrant theological framework, similar to if not exactly the same as the one I've described in this book. He begins with a "big view of creation" and an equally "cosmic view of sin." Then the meaning of God's becoming human in Jesus through his birth, life, death on the cross, and resurrection falls squarely within God's mission to "redeem and renew all things on earth, not just human souls. Culture—including popular culture—is in the middle of a massive redemption project while the world awaits Christ's return to earth to bring a culmination to it all."[15] Because of this, Heffner argues, we need eyes to see and hearts to discern the ways God is working redemption in all kinds of places, including in and through popular culture.[16]

Our family engaged with Harry Potter similarly. We learned of the series through other children, and our children wanted to read the books. We read them aloud and talked about the stories, very much expecting that they might be very good but not knowing how that would be true. As we saw the books turn darker, and the story line maturing with Harry as he grew year by year, we sometimes paused to read the next book at a later point. Yet we eagerly returned to the series, wondering about the fate of characters we grew to know and love (or despise, as the case may be). The books, like Lewis's *The Chronicles of Narnia*, are indeed about magic on the surface. They include frightful evil and violence but also wonderfully inspiring courage and love, as well as good fun. Yet they are told in such a way that they don't necessarily "preach" a message directly. Rather, as Rowan Williams has insightfully put it in referring to the writing of Flannery O'Connor, "She's somebody who, quite deliberately, doesn't set out to make the points that you might expect her to be making, but wants to build a world in which certain things may become plausible, or tangible, but not to get a message across."[17] A similar claim might be extended to J. K. Rowling in this masterful series.

We of course did not simply read the books and watch the movies. Much ink has been spilled reviewing, reveling in, and reviling the series. We've read our share of commentary, including some masterful analysis from Christian authors. Alan Jacobs's thoughtful writing has been one guide, and we have benefited from his comparison of Harry Potter to the penny dreadful–a cheap sort of kid's adventure novel of a century ago–that while not Christian were "always on the side of life."[18] Interestingly, this is true in one obvious sense: Harry is "the boy who lived," and Lord Voldemort leads his evil band of "death eaters," whose top goal is to kill Harry.

But in another sense, the novels help us see beyond this life, raising for us the expectation that this world of our daily lives is not all there is and that perhaps profound realities lie just around the corner of our understanding or perception.[19] I experience this in Luther Seminary's Chapel of the Cross, a space that has a soaring opening above the altar that is blocked from view by the line of the roof. Yet seven chains from seven candles above the altar draw the eyes upward, and during the day, light shines from the out-of-sight heights down toward the chapel. This simple architectural feature does, in a way, what platform 9¾ does in Harry Potter. While to the ordinary eye, nothing "more" is there, to the eyes of faith a whole world exists just on the other side, and that world is, in some respects, the life that is really life. I am not, of course, advocating any view that denigrates God's good creation. Yet as part of reality there is this "more" there all the time, and Harry Potter's world gives us a way to imagine this and enjoy it at the same time.

The point here is not to "Christianize" Harry Potter. Yet what we see "with" J. K. Rowling are aspects of life that are indeed what Christians know to be of deepest value. It is as though in reading the work, "your world has been expanded, your world has enlarged at the end of it," as Rowan Williams puts it.[20] Luke Bell, a Benedictine monk at Quarr Abbey, has written a masterful book about the Harry Potter series guided by this premise: "Christian faith speaks about what is most fundamental in the human condition. Good writing does the same, so it is to be expected that there is common ground."[21] His point in writing the book is in part to show that J. K. Rowling has written a series that, far from being the "devil's work," embodies some of the deepest values we Christians also hold, among them that the most powerful "magic" is self-giving love.[22]

SIGUR RÓS

A student came up to me one day after class and asked if I liked the Icelandic band Sigur Rós. Because I write about faith and pop culture, students assume I know about their favorite bands. I usually don't, but I really appreciate the gift of finding out about new and exciting music. "Well," the student continued, "you ought to check them out. They sing both in Icelandic and in a made-up language called 'hopelandic.'" This was early in 2010 and soon after Jónsi, the lead singer of the band, released a solo album (titled *Go*) and came through Minneapolis on tour. I didn't make it to the show, but my curiosity was piqued. Then a summer trip to Scandinavia (flying on Icelandic Air) gave me the chance to see their homeland, listen to their music, and watch (twice!) the remarkable film *Heima* ("at home" or "homeland" in Icelandic). *Heima* is a 2007 documentary film made at the end of a world tour. As they arrived home, the band decided to travel around Iceland performing a series of unannounced free concerts. The combination of the striking beauty of the landscape and its obvious connection to their equally beautiful music simply brought me up short. I had no words. I struggled to say what I found so exciting about the band. All I knew was that I needed to learn more.

When I arrived home from the trip, I bought the soundtrack from the film, *Hvarf-Heim*, a compilation of previously unreleased songs and live songs from the tour drawn from their four existing studio recordings. I listened to the album and began to learn something about the band. Sigur Rós consists of Jón Bor (Jónsi) Birgisson (vocals, guitars), Kjartan (Kjarri) Sveinsson (keyboards), Orri Páll Dýrason (drums), and Georg (Goggi) Hólm (bass). While this configuration took a few years to come together (they started in 1994 with Jónsi, Georg, and Ágúst Ævar Gunnarsson, the original drummer), by their second album, *Ágætis Byrjun* (1999), the foursome was set. After nearly two months of listening to their songs, I realized I loved their music and had no idea what, if anything, they were singing. The music took me somewhere. It wasn't so much a geographical sense of going some other place as much as it was perhaps opening up something "more" in the moment. It turns out I was not alone.

As I began to look into the band's story, I found that two Facebook fan pages echo this spiritual sense about the band. One, "Sigur

Rós Is My Religion," gives as the rationale, "Because everyone knows that listening to any album of theirs is, in fact, a spiritual experience."[23] This page borders on the typical fan worship of the band, but the second one clearly points elsewhere. Titled "And on the Seventh Day God Listened to Sigur Rós," this site clearly suggests a heavenly scent in the band's music.[24] Similarly, in an early review of their first single from *Ágætis Byrjun*, titled "Svefn-g-englar," a *Spin* magazine writer offered this overwrought description: "the sound of god weeping tears of gold in heaven."[25] While the band is not Christian or even religious in their self-definition, their music has consistently raised the issue of faith among critics and fans since their first album, *Von* ("hope").

They addressed the question of the spirituality in their music in a song-by-song interview for their third studio album, the 2005 *Takk* ("thanks" in Icelandic). Orri said, "We are not trying to be spiritual or anything. We are making music that moves people. Trying, you know, we want to do that. You know, that people get something out of it. Maybe that is spiritual?"[26] The band has a hard time describing their music. In one interview, they are asked a version of a question most interviewers have asked them: "What is the sound you are aiming for?" Georg answered, "All of our music just comes out and we never plan for anything special to happen but we always want to make it so that people will feel something when they hear it, to open up some flood gate."[27] Their music, often made in partnership with the Icelandic string quartet Amiina and other musicians, is something that emerges in an organic way. They never develop songs individually, choosing rather to come together and play, letting song ideas emerge from their jam sessions.

Some people have suggested that most of their songs have no lyrics. That is only partially true, I have learned. When their songs are in an emerging stage, Jónsi uses what he calls "some nonsense" vocals sung over the songs. They typically write the music first and only later consider lyrics. Because their first song, "Von," gave birth to this practice, they playfully named this nonsense style of singing as a language: Vonlenska ("hopelandic"). But they do eventually wrestle down lyrics too. Many of their songs have lyrics in Icelandic, although a good number have kept their earlier Vonlenska vocals. Vonlenska draws on the voice as an instrument, speaking in an emotional language rather than with actual lyrics and specific meaning. This fits their sense of themselves, leading with a vision of the soundscape they want to create. "Everything we do has a huge amount of soul, but no meaning," Jónsi said in a 2009 interview.[28] Paradoxical, I thought, since to have a huge amount of soul, one must imagine that the music itself has profound meaning. Later in that interview, Jónsi expressed a love of Washington Phillips, a gospel and blues singer from Texas whose mysterious life story and handful of recordings evoke the story of his contemporary Robert Johnson. Phillips apparently played an unusual instrument—a dulceola, celestaphone, or fretless zither, creating what Jónsi called an "amazing sound." Sigur Rós and Phillips share what the interviewer provocatively called "a fragile majesty."[29]

Such a phrase recalls the phrase that frames this book as a whole: broken hallelujahs. Such a sensibility, no doubt, is what allows the band a warm reception by people of faith. Ken Heffner invited the band to play at Calvin College in 2006. He created an open interview time before their concert, and the band was asked how they responded to their music being called "the soundtrack of heaven or music from God." The band laughed, acknowledging awareness of that reputation. They stated that they think about their music primarily in terms of beauty. To be regarded as music from God, they remarked, "is kind of a scary responsibility but also a cool thing." Heffner argued that the band has found a way to "tap into glory, to give glory a sound." Other musicians have done this, but at the moment, Heffner believes, Sigur Rós does it the best. "God is at work renewing all kinds of things and He can do it through a Sigur Rós concert" whether the artist intends this or not.[30]

Given this sort of reception by Christians, it is not surprising to hear that church leaders like Blaine Hogan of Willow Creek Community Church use Sigur Rós's songs as a soundtrack for worship. One example, a video for the "Act of Confession" in their worship, is based on the beautiful Sigur Rós song "Ára Bátur."[31] Ára Bátur is a highpoint for Sigur Rós, a major creative collaboration recorded live in the famous Abbey Road studio with the sixty-seven-piece London Sinfonietta and the twenty-strong London Oratory boys' choir. In typical form for a Sigur Rós song, "Ára Bátur" begins very quietly, with simple piano, and builds to a massive and moving crescendo with full orchestra and choir. The creative partnerships forged in this performance foreshadow the concert performed in November 2010 in New York City. In conjunction with the Lincoln Center's White Light Festival, Sigur Rós's keyboardist, Kjartan Sveinsson, and his bandmates performed his original work "Credo," along with other pieces. Collaborating with the Latvian Choir and the Wordless Music Orchestra, the concert took place in the Church of St. Paul the Apostle. Such an event gives just the most recent and dramatic example of why the band is called "postrock." It also shows why their hearers keep finding God at work in and through their art.[32] This version of "Credo" was not simply a setting of the Apostles' or Nicene Creeds traditionally included in musical settings of the mass. Rather, according to the program notes, Sveinsson wrote a piece combining Latin words representing things he believes in, but this personal creed was not printed lest others too easily take it for their own.[33] Drawing on a powerful historic form from the sung mass, performed in a church no less, offers the question for us to ponder: what do we believe? In their encouragement of this sort of reflection lyrically and musically, Sigur Rós in the end seems very near to Alan Jacobs's concluding judgment regarding J. K. Rowling's Harry Potter books: they are always on the side of life. "Above all," said Jónsi, "I'm grateful for the ability to compose music. Life is a gift."[34]

ARCADE FIRE

It ought to be admitted as I conclude with one final example that this book is deeply indebted to U2. That might sound slightly cloying, but I mean it honestly. There is simply too much new music, film, and other popular arts to pay attention to it all. The flood of cultural production and our accessibility to it has increased exponentially in the age of the internet. As with my student who told me about Sigur Rós, an extended Christian community figures here as a way of pointing out things worth engaging. U2 pointed me toward Leonard Cohen, encouraged me to explore the intersection of the blues and the psalms, and introduced me to Arcade Fire.

While Arcade Fire won the 2011 Record of the Year Grammy award for their third album, The Suburbs, in 2004 the band was little known. U2 gave them a bit of an early break, you might say.

During their Vertigo tour in 2005–6, the last song played over the PA before the band took the stage was Arcade Fire's "Wake Up" from their first full-length album, 2004's *Funeral*. "Wake Up" is a powerful song, arresting and cajoling the listener to wake up by sheer force of its musical energy. Without even seeing them play the song, I knew I had to find out more about this Canadian band.

I learned that many critics lauded *Funeral* as one of the best albums of the decade thus far (and it maintained this status as the decade-end lists were made).[35] Led by the husband-wife duo of Win Butler and Regine Chassagne, who met while in college in Montreal, the band had a number of early configurations of players before settling on a dynamic group of seven. Win Butler, a Texan, learned to play on a guitar given to him by his big-band leader grandfather Alvino Rey.[36] Regine Chassagne, who grew up in an expatriate Haitian family living in Montreal, was in college before she began playing music (playing recorder in a medieval music group). Through 2003, in fits and starts, they were joined by an experienced group of musician friends. Richard Reed Parry and Sarah Neufeld were playing in Bell Orchestre, while Tim Kinsbury and Jeremy Gara were playing with Parry in The New Internationals. Win's younger brother Will got involved while on break from college, and the band was set. The combination of challenging ideas, musical virtuosity, and passionate performance has made the band a live favorite and has sparked their rise over the last decade.

Funeral was a particularly intense record because of the fact that no less than nine family members of the band died during the writing and recording of the album. One song, "Une Annee Sans Lumiere" ("a year without light") seemingly summarizes the emotional space of the band during that period. Yet rather than wallow in sorrow, the album is also a statement about maturity and grasping onto life lived to its fullest.[37] "Wake Up," of course, captures this sensibility. It was written as a bombastic song to start their concerts but now, after becoming a huge fan favorite, regularly ends their shows.

As news of a second album began to emerge, my interest grew deeper. I learned that the band had purchased the Petite Église in Farnham (about an hour outside Montreal), turned it into a recording studio, and had recorded a religious album.[38] Titled *Neon Bible*, the band's sophomore album picked up musically where *Funeral* left off but took a decidedly prophetic turn in its lyrics. In one of the best articles on the band, written just after *Neon Bible* was released in 2007, Paul Morley of the UK's Guardian newspaper describes the group as "a scholarly post-punk gospel choir merrily identifying the menace of the world."[39]

Indeed, written in the era of the George W. Bush's "war on terror," *Neon Bible* was a passionate and bitter pill delivered in creative and musically dynamic form. The title song, "Neon Bible," begins with the unmistakable buzzing hum of a neon sign. The band actually commissioned a six-foot neon bible, used on tour and portrayed on the cover of the album. The song portrays our age as media-infatuated, idolizing a "neon bible" of television and computers, losing ourselves "in the light of a golden calf" to which we turn for truth (clearly referencing Exod. 32). Arcade Fire beg to differ: "Not much chance for survival, if the Neon Bible is right." The critique is of religion, but as with biblical prophecy, it is not antireligious but is, rather, faithful critique of the abuse of religion. *Neon Bible*, lead singer Win Butler says, "is addressing religion in a way that only someone who actually cares about it can."[40]

Although the Butler brothers grew up in a Mormon family and Win studied religion at McGill University, the album is not conventionally religious. Yet its songs are haunted by religious questions and, if one is careful in listening, religious convictions that seem oriented to life, if not traditional Christianity. "Intervention," the fifth song on the album, is an interesting case in point. "It's like a hymn," according to Win Butler.[41] It begins with Regine playing the organ (from St-Jean Baptiste in Montreal) with all stops pulled.[42] Building on the bombast only a pipe organ could provide, the song includes full orchestra backing the already multi-instrumentalist band members. The song begins, "The king's taken back the throne," a poetic nod to President Bush's reelection. The second verse portrays the struggle of soldiers fighting "though nothing's on the line," pressing toward a critical commentary on the endless (and by many accounts needless) war in Iraq.[43]

With this ominous beginning, it is easier to make sense of the curious chorus that includes the line, "working for the church while your family dies." This line, repeated multiple times, led to the widely held but mistaken view that is was a song about the church. It is, of a sort, but America is the "church," which asks the ultimate allegiance from its "members." The bitter chorus continues, "You take what they give you and you keep it inside." It is a song that highlights the potential for good by focusing on how religion goes wrong. In the concluding version of the chorus, the line is "Singin' hallelujah with the fear in your heart." Win suggested in an interview that the album is about "two kinds of fear: the Bible talks a lot about fear of God–fear in the face of something awesome. That kind of fear is the type that makes someone want to change. But a fear of other people makes you want to stay the same, to protect what you have. It's a stagnant fear; and it's paralyzing."[44] As a song, "Intervention" might be a prophetic intervention crying out against leadership driven by the second sort of fear. Win opened up about the band's protest: "If you feel something is wrong, you shouldn't be silent."[45]

Even more interesting as a sign of the album's complex commentary on religion was the band's decision to play a series of album release concerts hosted by churches: St. John's Church, Westminster, London, and Judson Memorial Church in New York City. The last of the five sold out New York City concerts was live-streamed on NPR, a jubilant and powerful night despite the bleakness of some of the songs. Typical of the band, after the encore they snuck out a side door to play an acoustic version of "Wake Up" for unsuspecting fans milling about outside. One attendee reported, "It's a scene of communion that feels in direct opposition to *Neon Bible's* estrangement: a hundred people trying so hard together to remember these seconds." This sense of communion emerges from the intensity of their creative work together.

The brothers (Win and Will) and the husband–wife duo (Win and Regine) help ground a community orientation. Regine: "Our togetherness is what makes us special. It's what feeds into the music, and I think people can feel that, that it is important to us because it is our life, not just our career."[46] Despite Regine and Win writing most songs, the band shares credit for songwriting and arranging, an acknowledgment of their communal work ethic and commitment to equality. This translates from the studio to the stage, where it is the exception for any one band member to play the same instrument throughout a show, and often the band will flip-flop instruments from song to song or even within a song. That passionate energy has become a hallmark of the band, and it takes its toll. (Will recalls a line of bruises running up his arm from overenthusiastic tambourine bashing.)[47]

The shared commitment to the life of the band has also translated into major support for Regine's homeland of Haiti. They have actively worked against the extreme poverty of that island nation, especially in the wake of the devastating earthquake of January 2010. Despite being on tour in support of the band's most recent and most successful album, *The Suburbs*, some of the band, including Regine and Win, went to Haiti to volunteer with Partners in Health, an organization the band has supported from early on. They dedicated a dollar from every ticket to every show of the tour, raising a million dollars for work in Haiti. They have consistently been ambassadors for Haiti, speaking to audiences in support of relief and development aid. While they had for many years rejected out of hand any proposals to license their songs for advertizing, when the USA's Super Bowl offered a quarter million dollars for the rights to use "Wake Up" in 2011, they said yes. "That offer came in literally the day after the earthquake. There's a point at which it's immoral not to do it. Cos otherwise they're gonna use someone else's song and the money's not gonna go to Haiti."[48]

Arcade Fire, then, repays the practice of surrender by opening up avenues of reflection on some of the issues that matter most in life—who we serve with our lives, how we live, love, and create with the gifts we have been given, and what is worth fighting for and against. Their depth of passion as musicians is driven by their passion for ideas, including the core idea that life is to be lived fully, awake, and with deep concern for the lives of others, whether it be their fellow band members, their fans, or the very poorest people in the world today. All of this exuberance of life seemed to be channeled into their biggest concert to date—headlining the Southern California Coachella festival in May of 2011. As their fifteen-song set closed, Win belted out, "This is our last song, so I want you to sing it really loud." The insistent drum and violin signaled the song, and within seconds, tens of thousands of fans were shouting along with the band. Then large balls came pouring over the top of the stage, becoming a huge mass of bouncing joy throughout the crowd. But then, almost in sync with the band, the orbs began to glow in blue, purple, pink, red, green, and violet, and the energy that had peaked at a roar rose a few notches more. The faces of the band were clearly caught up in the joy of the moment, a communion of immense proportions that seemed to be the fully realized possibility of rock-and-roll concerts to take people outside of themselves and touch something larger, something that may just be very good indeed.

I fully expect that if you have persevered to the end of this book, then you will have already begun thinking of your own engagement with pop culture. Case studies are ready at hand. I hope you will engage the intersections of faith and pop culture with a small group using the study guide created to provoke further thinking along the trajectory sketched out in the previous chapters. The journey of surrender embodied in miniature here in this final chapter gives concrete shape to what C. S. Lewis named as an enlargement—and ultimately a "healing"—of the self. I have followed his lead in sketching that enlargement in the shape of the cross, a life of generosity and loving attention, trusting that in such encounters I am meeting the height and breadth and depth of God refracted through the full stretch of living—from the cry of abandonment to the cry of joy. To that living we turn now, having journeyed this way together. For that journey, and that which is to come, I give thanks.

NOTES

Chapter 1 The Seductiveness of Certainty

1. *Paste* has been a mainstay of my pop culture engagement since this introduction. See www.pastemagazine.com.

2. Christian Scharen, *One Step Closer: Why U2 Matters to Those Seeking God* (Grand Rapids: Brazos, 2006).

3. The line is from U2, "Stand Up Comedy," *No Line On The Horizon* (Interscope, 2009), track seven.

4. While I don't defend a particular understanding of pop culture, I mean the straightforward sense that something is popular; that is, lots of people like it, buy it, watch it, and that as such it justifies close theological reflection. For a more in-depth engagement with various understandings of popular culture (as opposed to "high" culture, "folk" culture, or a form of resistance against "dominant" culture), see Gordon Lynch, *Understanding Theology and Popular Culture* (New York: Blackwell, 2005). Also see Kelton Cobb, *The Blackwell Guide to Theology and Popular Culture* (New York: Blackwell, 2005); and William D. Romanowski, *Eyes Wide Open: Looking for God in Popular Culture* (Grand Rapids: Brazos, 2007).

5. An obvious example would be the Recording Industry Association of America's parental advisory label for "explicit lyrics" or the Motion Picture Association of America's familiar rating system (G, PG, PG-13, R, and NC-17). The Entertainment Software Rating Board manages a similar rating system for video games (EC, E, E10+, T, M, and A).

6. Randall Balmer and Lauren F. Winner, *Protestantism in America* (New York: Columbia University Press, 2005), 43.

7. You can read the full interview at www.christianbook.com/Christian/Books/cms_content?page=1146698&event=ESRCN.

8. In addition to this book and *One Step Closer*, an accessible understanding of a theology of the cross can be found in Andrew Root, *The Promise of Despair* (Nashville: Abingdon, 2010); Douglas John Hall, *The Cross in Our Context* (Minneapolis: Fortress, 2003); Gerhard Forde, *On Being a Theologian of the Cross* (Grand Rapids: Eerdmans, 1997).

9. Philip Yancey, *What's So Amazing about Grace?* (Grand Rapids: Zondervan, 1997).

10. U2's song "Playboy Mansion," from the 1997 album *Pop*, is one of the most playful odes to grace ever to be written, and my sentences here draw on that song, written during the era Bono had taken a great liking to Yancey's book.

11. See Eric Gritsch and Robert Jenson, *Lutheranism: The Theological Movement and Its Confessional Writings* (Philadelphia: Fortress, 1976), 42–44.

12. The classic formulation might be put this way: that although we are broken and sinful, we offer up our failures and brokenness to Jesus, who takes them and in return gives us his own righteousness or, perhaps better, draws us into his own life, covering us with his love and forgiveness.

13. For a recent thoughtful examination of the way these contradictions in Johnny Cash's life connect to contradictions present in America's dominant culture, see Rodney Clapp, *Johnny Cash and the American Contradiction: Christianity and the Battle for the Soul of a Nation* (Louisville: Westminster John Knox, 2008).

14. Kim Lawton, "Bono Unplugged," *Religion and Ethics Newsweekly*, February 3, 2006, http://www.pbs.org/wnet/religionandethics/week923/exclusive.html.

15. Not to mention bordering on the ancient heresy of Manichaeism, which views the material world as a world of darkness and evil. For a good overview of this and related dualist beliefs and their impact on Christianity, see Yuri Stoyanov, *The Other God: Dualist Religions from Antiquity to the Cathar Heresy* (New Haven: Yale University Press, 2000).

16. Scharen, *One Step Closer*, 11.

Chapter 2 The Holy and the Broken Hallelujah

1. Leonard Cohen, "Boogie Street," in *Book of Longing* (New York: HarperCollins, 2006), 64.

2. "*Book of Longing:* Interview with Leonard Cohen," *Fresh Air*, WHYY, May 22, 2006. Interview available at www.npr.org/templates/story/story.php?storyId=5422403.

3. Nick Paton Walsh, "Interview with Leonard Cohen," *Observer*, Oct. 14, 2001.

4. "Anthem" from 1992's *The Future*: "I think it is one of the best songs I have written, maybe the best. It's up there with "If It Be Your Will" and "Take This Waltz." It is saying there is a crack in everything–forget about your perfect offering. I knew that song was everything that my whole work and life had somehow gathered around. It is absolutely true to me." Robert Hilburn, "A Master's Reflections on His Music," *Los Angeles Times*, September 24, 1995.

5. Leonard Cohen, "You Don't Want to Go Out Anymore," in *Book of Longing*, 135.

6. Leonard Cohen, "My Time," in *Book of Longing*, 178.

7. Ira B. Nadel, *Various Positions: A Life of Leonard Cohen* (Austin: University of Texas Press, 1996), 13.

8. Ibid., 44.

9. Ibid, 126.

10. David Boucher, *Dylan and Cohen: Poets of Rock and Roll* (New York: Continuum, 2004), 219.

11. Ibid., 194.

12. Nadel, *Various Positions*, 215.

13. Ibid., 214.

14. Ibid., 272.

15. Ibid., 272–73.

16. Leonard Cohen, interviewed for Norwegian Radio by Kari Hesthamar, "Leonard Looks Back on the Past," www.leonardcohenfiles.com/leonard2006.html.

17. Lian Lunson, *Leonard Cohen: I'm Your Man* (Santa Monica: Lionsgate Films, 2006), my transcription.

18. Nadel, *Various Positions*, 155.

19. Hestamar, "Leonard Looks Back on the Past."

20. Ibid.

21. Nadel, *Various Positions,* 237.

22. Ibid, 238.

23. Ibid.

24. Ibid., 239.

25. Ibid., 151.

26. Ibid, 241.

27. Leonard Cohen, "Leonard Cohen as Interviewed by Robert Sward," Montreal Quebec, 1984, www.leonardcohenfiles.com/sward.html.

28. Leonard Cohen, *Book of Mercy* (Toronto: McClelland & Stewart, 1984), prayer 15. The book was published with no page numbers and no titles for the fifty poems other than numbers at the top of each poem. Each is clearly written as a prayer, and so I reference them as "prayer" and the number.

29. Nadel, *Various Positions*, 241.

30. Cohen, *Book of Mercy*, prayer 6.

31. Cohen, *Book of Mercy*, prayer 5.

32. Hesthamar, "Leonard Looks Back on the Past."

33. Nadel, *Various Positions*, 239.

34. Cohen in Sward interview.

35. Cohen, *Book of Mercy*, prayer 19.

36. Ibid., prayer 49.

37. Boucher, *Dylan and Cohen*, 220.

38. Hesthamar, "Leonard Looks Back on the Past."

39. Interview with Leonard Cohen, the *Mike Walsh Show*, the Nine television network (Australia), May 1985, quoted in http://en.wikipedia.org/wiki/Dance_Me_to_the_End_of_Love.

40. Nadel, *Various Positions*, 159. His childhood in Catholic Montreal, and his young adult fascination with Blessed Catherine Tekakwitha, an Iroquois girl converted by the Jesuits in the seventeenth century, help account for his exposure to and interest in Christian themes. Tekakwitha was the inspiration for his 1966 novel *Beautiful Losers*, a novel described both as utter trash and as a meditation on saintliness.

41. Hesthamar, "Leonard Looks Back on the Past."

42. "Dylan and I were having coffee in Paris a few years ago. He was doing 'Hallelujah' in concert and asked how long it took to write. I said, 'Oh, the best part of two years.' He said, 'Two years?' Kinda shocked. And then we started talking about a song of his called 'I and I.' I said, 'How long did it take you to write that?' He said, 'Oh, best part of 15 minutes.' I almost fell off my chair. And the thing is I lied. Actually, it took me closer to five years. Of course he lied, too. It probably took him 10 minutes." "Leonard Cohen: His Wit, Warmth, and Wisdom," *Telegraph,* June 14, 2008.

43. The reference here is to a best-selling book by popular Houston-based preacher Joel Osteen, *Your Best Life Now: 7 Steps to Living at your Full Potential* (New York: Faithword, 2004).

44. Hilburn, "A Master's Reflections on His Music."

45. Ibid.

Chapter 3 Why God Loves the Blues

1. "What a Little Moonlight Can Do" was written by Harry M. Woods in 1934 and recorded by Billie Holiday in 1935 as one of her first single records.

2. This account is pulled from numerous sources, including Billie Holiday, *Lady Sings the Blues*, with William Duffy (1956; repr., New York: Penguin, 1992), 84; and Donald Clarke, *Wishing on the Moon* (Cambridge, MA: Da Capo Press, 2000), 164.

3. The best examination of this lynching is James H. Madison, *A Lynching in the Heartland: Race and Memory in America* (New York: Palgrave Macmillan, 2003).

4. Holiday, *Lady Sings the Blues*, 84; Angela Davis, *Blues Legacies and Black Feminism: Gertrude "Ma" Rainey, Bessie Smith and Billie Holiday* (New York: Random House, 1998), 186.

5. Robert O'Meally, *Lady Day: The Many Faces of Billie Holiday* (Cambridge, MA: Da Capo Press, 1991), 136.

6. Holiday, *Lady Sings the Blues*, 119.

7. Meg Green, *Billie Holiday: A Biography* (Westport, CT: Greenwood Press, 2007), 61.

8. David Margolick, *Strange Fruit: The Biography of a Song* (New York: Harper, 2001), 59.

9. Ibid., 7.

10. Ibid., 29.

11. Ibid, 56.

12. Incredibly, after the horror of 4,742 recorded lynchings in American history, and undoubtedly more that were unrecorded, the Senate could not even achieve an on-the-record unanimous vote. In fact, the 2005 vote was a voice vote, so individual votes would not be recorded, and was cosponsored by eighty of one hundred senators, a surprising tally. "It's a statement in itself that there aren't one hundred cosponsors," said Senator John Kerry (D-Mass.). Sheryl Gay Stolberg, "Senate Issues Apology over Failure on Lynching Law," *New York Times*, June 14, 2005, www.nytimes.com/2005/06/14/politics/14lynch.html.

13. Wynton Marsalis, audio excerpt from *Jazz: A Film by Ken Burns*, www.pbs.org/jazz/biography/artist_id_holiday_billie.htm.

14. A video of this famous performance is available on YouTube, www.youtube.com/watch?v=sXRYdcQ6bbM.

15. "Just One of Those Things," written by Cole Porter for the 1935 musical *Jubilee*, was recorded by Billie Holiday on Verve Records in 1957.

16. Davis, *Blues Legacies and Black Feminism*, 193.

17. Holiday, *Lady Sings the Blues*, 84; Davis, *Blues Legacies and Black Feminism*, 195.

18. Dave Headlam, "Does the Song Remain the Same? Questions of Authenticity and Identification in the Music of Led Zeppelin," in *Concert Music, Rock, and Jazz since 1945: Essays and Analytical Studies*, ed. Elizabeth West Marvin and Richard Hermann (Rochester, NY: University of Rochester Press, 1996), 313–63.

19. See, for example, www.en.wikipedia.org/wiki/The_Yardbirds.

20. "Eric Clapton Takes on Robert Johnson's Blues," *Morning Edition*, March 30, 2004, www.npr.org/templates/story/story.php?storyId=1798862.

21. "Eric Clapton Visits CNN's *Larry King Live*," February 13, 1998, www.eric-clapton.co.uk/interviewsandarticles/kinginterview.htm.

22. Jon Michael Spencer, *Blues and Evil* (Knoxville: University of Tennessee, 1993), xii.

23. Paul Oliver, *Blues Fell This Morning: Meaning in the Blues* (Cambridge: Cambridge University Press, 1994 [1960]), 117.

24. Spencer, *Blues and Evil*, xii.

25. Giles Oakley, *The Devil's Music: A History of the Blues*, 2nd ed. (New York: Da Capo Press, 1997 [1976]), 8.

26. For more, see Peter Guralnick, *Searching for Mr. Johnson* (New York: Penguin, 1989); Elijah Wald, *Escaping the Delta: Robert Johnson and the Invention of the Blues* (New York: HarperCollins, 2004).

27. Spencer, *Blues and Evil*, xiii.

28. Ibid., 10.

29. Ibid., 10–11.

30. Ibid., 99.

31. The first track on the Rolling Stones 1968 album *Beggars Banquet*.

32. Spencer, *Blues and Evil*, xv.

33. Alan Lomax, " 'Sinful' Songs of the Southern Negro," in *Selected Writings, 1934–1997*, ed. Ronald D. Cohen (New York: Routledge, 2003), 10.

34. Oliver, *Blues Fell This Morning*, 122.

35. Not much is known about Smith, alternately known as John T. Smith, The Howling Wolf, Funny Papa, or Funny Paper Smith. He traveled through Texas in the 1920s and 1930s. Only one of his recording sessions–from 1930–31–has survived. He was a rough character, and his blues career ended when he was imprisoned for murder and died in jail.

36. Oliver, *Blues Fell This Morning*, 117–18.

37. Ibid.

38. W. E. B. Du Bois, *The Souls of Black Folk* (New York: Pocket Books, 2005), 7. "It is a peculiar sensation, this double-consciousness, this sense of always looking at one's self through the eyes of others, of measuring one's soul by the tape of a world that looks on in amused contempt and pity. One ever feels his two-ness–an American, a Negro; two souls, two thoughts, two unreconciled strivings; two warring ideals in one dark body, whose dogged strength alone keeps it from being torn asunder."

39. Davis, *Blues Legacies and Black Feminism*, 93.

40. Jon Michael Spencer, *Protest and Praise: Sacred Music of Black Religion* (Minneapolis: Fortress, 1990), 122.

41. Ibid., 123.

42. Du Bois, *Souls of Black Folk*, 251.

43. James Cone, *The Spirituals and the Blues: An Interpretation* (Maryknoll, NY: Orbis, 1992), 100.

44. Ibid., 100.

45. Ibid., 103.

46. The best engagement with the Saturday night–Sunday morning conflict and connection is Don and Emily Saliers, *A Song to Sing, A Life to Live: Reflections on Music as Spiritual Practice* (San Francisco: Jossey-Bass, 2004), 153–68.

47. For example, Robert Palmer's classic book *Deep Blues* (New York: Viking, 1981) mentions Rainey and Smith once each, while dedicating many pages each to Son House, Robert Johnson, Muddy Waters, and later blues luminaries.

48. The happy exception is Stephen Nichols, a professor of Christianity and culture at Lancaster Bible College. I have learned a good deal from his

excellent book *Getting the Blues: What Blues Music Teaches Us about Suffering and Salvation* (Grand Rapids: Brazos, 2008).

49. Sandra Lieb, *Mother of the Blues: A Study of Ma Rainey* (Amherst: University of Massachusetts Press, 1983), 3.

50. When minstrel shows burst on the scene in the 1840s, they were led by whites who blackened their faces and used grotesque physical exaggeration to mimic slave life on the plantation. Within twenty years, however, very successful black minstrels appeared, moderating the exaggerated parody while maintaining the humor and good music. Officially billed as "Madame Gertrude" for the tent shows, Rainey was among the most popular entertainers of this era. See Lieb, *Mother of the Blues*, 7.

51. N. Lee Orr, "Gertrude 'Ma' Rainey (1886–1939)," in *The New Georgia Encyclopedia*, www.georgiaencyclopedia.org/nge/Article.jsp?id=h-876.

52. Spencer, *Blues and Evil*, 35.

53. Lieb, *Mother of the Blues*, 27.

54. Ibid., 30, from her interview with Dorsey.

55. Ibid., xvi.

56. All of Ma Rainey's lyrics are carefully transcribed and published in Davis, *Blues Legacies and Black Feminism*, with "Misery Blues" on 233–34.

57. Ibid., lyrics on 238.

58. Ibid., 17–18.

59. Lieb, *Mother of the Blues*, 16.

60. Davids, *Blues Legacies and Black Feminism*, 128.

61. Ibid.

62. Ibid., 129.

63. August Wilson, *Ma Rainey's Black Bottom* (New York: Penguin, 1985), 83.

64. Michael W. Harris, *The Rise of the Gospel Blues: The Music of Thomas Andrew Dorsey in the Urban Church* (New York: Oxford University Press, 1992), 22.

65. Ibid., xx.

66. Ibid., 31. "If I heard a new song at the theater or a party, I would come home and sit at the organ till I could play it that very night. If it was 10 o'clock when I got home, or 11 o'clock, I'd go home; I'd play it, pick it out, practice it at night before going to bed."

67. Ibid., 70.

68. Ibid., 96.

69. Ibid., 82.

70. Daniel Alexander Payne, *Recollections of Seventy Years* (Nashville: AME Sunday School Union, 1888), 93–94.

71. Harris, *The Rise of the Gospel Blues*, 148.

72. Ibid., 148–49.

73. Ibid., 150.

74. Transcribed from spoken introduction to "Precious Lord" on Thomas A. Dorsey, *Recordings of the Great Gospel Songs of Thomas A. Dorsey* (Sony Entertainment, 1973).

75. Harris, *Rise of the Gospel Blues*, 239.

76. Ibid., 97.

77. Mahalia Jackson was a protégé of Dorsey and frequently sang at civil rights gatherings just before Dr. Martin Luther King Jr. spoke. This was the case at the famous March on Washington speech in August of 1963. She was there at his funeral as well, singing his favorite song. See Craig Werner, *Change Is Gonna Come: Music, Race and the Soul of America* (New York: Plume, 1999), 9.

78. Spencer, *Protest and Praise*, 122.

79. The echo of Romans 8:26 is unmistakable: "God does our praying in and for us, making prayer out of our wordless sighs, our aching groans."

80. Adam Block, "Pure Bono," *Mother Jones*, May 1989, p. 35.

Chapter 4 Cries

1. Don Saliers, "Beauty and Terror," *Spiritus: A Journal of Christian Spirituality* 2, no. 2 (Fall 2002): 181–91.

2. See, for example, David Jones and Russell Woodbridge, *Health, Wealth and Happiness: Has the Prosperity Gospel Overshadowed the Gospel of Christ?* (Grand Rapids: Kregel, 2011).

3. Bruce Wilkinson's *The Prayer of Jabez: Breaking through to the Blessed Life* (Portland: Multnomah, 2000) has sold more than nine million copies and spawned an industry of follow-up media seeking to capitalize on its success. Rodney Clapp and John Wright, in their critical article "God as Santa: Misreading the Prayer of Jabez," raise serious questions about how Wilkinson displaces the Lord's Prayer as the central prayer for Christians and unpack some of the consequences that follow. See *Christian Century*, October 23, 2002, reprinted at www.religion-online.org/Showarticle.asp?title=2623.

4. David F. Ford, *Christian Wisdom: Desiring God and Learning in Love*, Cambridge Studies in Christian Doctrine (New York: Cambridge University Press, 2007), 4–5.

5. Ibid., 51.

6. Ibid.; see also Bernd Wannenwetsch, *Political Worship* (New York: Oxford University Press, 2004), 202.

7. So his lecture, "That Majestic Theme," Midwinter Convocation, Luther Seminary, St. Paul, January 14, 2009; see also Walter Brueggemann, *The Psalms and the Life of Faith*, ed. Patrick D. Miller (Minneapolis: Fortress, 1995), 106.

8. See Terence E. Fretheim, *Exodus*, Interpretation: A Bible Commentary for Teaching and Preaching (Louisville: Westminster John Knox, 1991), 24–25.

9. Ibid., 30.

10. Laurel Dykstra, *Set Them Free: The Other Side of Exodus* (Maryknoll, NY: Orbis, 2002).

11. Andrew Root, "If the Truth Were Told: Fox TV's 'Moment of Truth,'" *Christian Century*, August 12, 2008.

12. Renita J. Weems, "The Hebrew Women Are Not Like the Egyptian Women: The Ideology of Race, Gender and Sexual Reproduction in Exodus 1," *Semeia* 59 (1992): 29.

13. Dykstra, *Set Them Free*, 163–64.

14. Dykstra's reflections on divine violence are worth reading: ibid., 128–45. It is interesting that the women don't resort to violence but engage in nonviolent civil disobedience. Moses (and, like him, God) does. See also Peter C. Craigie, *The Problem of War in the Old Testament* (Grand Rapids: Eerdmans, 1978), 67–68.

15. Patrick D. Miller, *They Cried to the Lord: The Form and Theology of Biblical Prayer* (Minneapolis: Fortress, 1994).

16. On the issues of Matthew's relation to Jewish communities in the first century and its shaping of his story of Jesus, I have learned most from Daniel Harrington, SJ, *The Gospel of Matthew* (Collegeville, MN: Liturgical Press, 1991).

17. Rowan Williams, *The Wound of Knowledge*, 2nd ed. (Boston: Cowley, 2003), 13.

18. Ibid., 14.

19. Ibid.

20. This way of Jesus belongs to God "as he is in himself," for in Jesus we have God's "very self and essence all divine." Thus, Jesus's "invitation to the outcast is not adequately seen as a mere parable of the divine invitation, but rather as its actuality become event." Here it becomes clear that one needs to take the notion of kenosis and all it represents for Jesus's birth, life, and death on the cross "back into the initiating act of the whole incarnate life." Donald MacKinnon, "*Kenosis* and Establishment," in *The Stripping of the Altars* (New York: Collins, 1969), 24.

Chapter 5 Grace and Karma

1. Heather Clark, "Mother Charged after Toddler's Body Is Found Buried in Sand at Playground," *Minneapolis Star Tribune*, May 22, 2009, A7.

2. Ibid.

3. Reviewing interviews with forty women in prison who killed their children, scholars Michelle Oberman and Cheryl Meyer show that "the common themes that emerge in each of these women's stories include domestic violence, troubled relationships with parents, twisted notions of romantic love and deep conflicts about motherhood. Even more pervasive is how many of these women were failed by the social and institutional systems set up to detect and defuse problems before they become tragedies." See *When Mothers Kill:*

Interviews from Prison (New York: New York University Press, 2008). Quote from *Publishers Weekly* review of the book, accessed online at www.amazon.com/When-Mothers-Kill-Interviews-Ancient/dp/0814757022/ref=sr_1_1?s=books&ie=UTF8&qid=1308749851&sr-1-1.

4. Andrew Root's *The Promise of Despair* (Nashville: Abingdon, 2010) outlines a range of disquieting minideaths that cause despair–from divorce to loss of a job to cancer–and portrays a theological response to them that has much in common with the theological claims I argue for here.

5. H. Richard Niebuhr, *Christ and Culture* (New York: Harper and Row, 1951).

6. Dan Gilgoff, *The Jesus Machine: How James Dobson, Focus on the Family, and Evangelical America Are Winning the Culture War* (New York: St. Martin's Press, 2008), 42.

7. The church's website lists an official statement of beliefs for the Church of the Nazarene (www.nazarene.org/ministries/administration/visitorcenter/display.aspx); for an excellent recent work on Christian faith from a Nazarene perspective, see Samuel M. Powell, *Discover Our Christian Faith: An Introduction to Theology* (Kansas City: Beacon Hill Press, 2008).

8. Gilgoff, *The Jesus Machine*, 21.

9. James Dobson, *Dare to Discipline* (Carol Stream, IL: Tyndale, 1970).

10. Gilgoff, *Jesus Machine*, 42.

11. Steve Rabey, "For Giant Evangelical Ministry, Midlife Crisis at 25," *New York Times* July 27, 2002, www.nytimes.com/2002/07/27/nyregion/religion-journal-for-giant-evangelical-ministry-midlife-crisis-at-25.html?pagewanted=1.

12. Tim Stafford, "A Demanding Doctor," *Christianity Today* 50, no. 4 (April 2006): 103.

13. "Trial Opens on Sale of 2 Live Crew Album," *New York Times*, October 2, 1990, www.nytimes.com/1990/10/02/us/trial-opens-on-sale-of-2-live-crew-album.html?pagewanted=1.

14. James Dobson, "Does Every Generation Think Their Kid's Music Has Gone Too Far?" http://family.custhelp.com/cgi-bin/family.cfg/php/enduser/popup_adp.php?p_faqid=945&p_created=1043958495.

15. Ted Slater, "Plugged In and R-rated Movies," on The Line blog, www.boundlessline.org/2008/06/plugged-in-and.html.

16. Ibid.

17. Ibid.

18. Adam Holz, "Christian Metal Bands: The Holy Growl," Focus on the Family, http://www.focusonthefamily.com/entertainment/mediawise/christian-metal-bands-the-holy-growl.aspx.

19. Given the content of the song, it is remarkable that the choir singing the song from which West samples was the Addicts Rehabilitation Center Gospel Choir (Curtis Lundy director). The album containing the song, titled "Walk with Me," was released in June 1997 by Mapleshade Records.

20. www.pluggedin.com/music/albums/2004/kanyewest-thecollegedropout .aspx.

21. See C. S. Lewis, "Meditation in a Toolshed," in *God in the Dock: Essays on Theology and Ethics* (Grand Rapids: Eerdmans, 1994), 212–15. Paul L. Holmer's book on C. S. Lewis has been immensely helpful here and on many other points. See *C. S. Lewis: The Shape of His Faith and Thought* (New York: Harper and Row, 1976), 71–72.

22. Holmer, *C. S. Lewis*, 94.

23. Ibid., 63.

24. John Lennon's song "Instant Karma!" was the third track on his 1975 solo album *Shaved Fish* (Apple/EMI Records).

25. A classic text here is Louis Dumont, *Homo Hierarchicus: The Caste System and Its Implications* (Chicago: University of Chicago Press, 1980).

26. Technically, Wesley argues for a preparing grace that prepares us to hear what Christ has done; a justifying grace that we grasp hold of in faith and that saves us from sin, death, and the devil; and a sanctifying grace that by the Holy Spirit helps us toward "Christian perfection" even while relapsing into sin and losing salvation remains a real possibility. See Randy Maddox, *Responsible Grace: John Wesley's Practical Theology* (Nashville: Abindgon, 1994).

27. Mary Douglas has been particularly effective at engaging these dynamics. See especially *Purity and Danger: An Analysis of the Concepts of Pollution and Taboo* (London: Routledge and Kegan Paul, 1966).

28. See, for example, "John Winthrop's *City upon a Hill, 1630*," reproduced at Mount Holyoke's website, www.mtholyoke.edu/acad/intrel/winthrop.htm.

29. Examples abound, but a classic in the literature is President Ronald Reagan in the 1980s describing the Soviet Union as the "Evil Empire," language taken as much from the Bible as from the *Star Wars* movie franchise so popular through the 1970s and 1980s.

30. Rowan Williams, *Tokens of Trust: An Introduction to Christian Belief* (Louisville: Westminster John Knox, 2010), 35.

31. Tim Keller, *The Prodigal God: Recovering the Heart of the Christian Faith* (New York: Dutton, 2008).

32. C. S. Lewis, *Letters to Malcom: Chiefly on Prayer* (1963; repr., New York: Harcourt, 1991), 73.

33. Charles Taylor, *A Secular Age* (Cambridge, Mass.: Harvard University Press, 2007), 115, 741.

34. U2 put it well in the classic anthem "Sunday, Bloody Sunday": rather than trenches of conflict dug between the two sides of the battle, the band describes "trenches dug within our hearts." See their 1983 album *War* (Island Records).

Chapter 6 Surrender to the Music

1. Holz cites a study by pollster MarketCast that found that the people who described themselves as "very religious" were just about as likely to see a

movie that was rated R for sexual content as those who described themselves as "nonreligious."

2. *Glory*, a 1989 film directed by Edward Zwick, told the story of the 54th Massachusetts Volunteer Infantry, the Civil War's first African American infantry division.

3. See Ted Slater, "*Plugged-In* and R-Rated Movies," June 12, 2008, www .boundlessline.org/2008/06/plugged-in-and.html.

4. Craig Detweiler and Barry Taylor, *A Matrix of Meanings: Finding God in Pop Culture* (Grand Rapids: Baker Academic, 2003). The book leads a series titled Engaging Culture, edited by William Dyrness and Robert K. Johnston, which is "designed to help Christians respond with theological discernment to our contemporary culture."

5. C. S. Lewis, *An Experiment in Criticism* (Cambridge: Cambridge University Press, 1961), 19.

6. Detweiler and Taylor, *Matrix of Meanings*, 16.

7. For a really interesting engagement with this idea of "common grace," see Theodore A. Turnau III, "Reflecting Theologically on Popular Culture as Meaningful: The Role of Sin, Grace, and General Revelation," *Calvin Theological Journal* 37 (2002): 270–96.

8. Detweiler and Taylor, *Matrix of Meanings*, 16.

9. Ibid., 10.

10. Ibid., 296. We'll see as the argument of the chapter unfolds that this is most definitely not Lewis's argument. Rather, his robust theological perspective grounds a certain kind of posture toward the world that both knows of God's presence already at work in the world and has been shaped by God's work in us. So, rather than looking to pop culture to "rethink, reform, reinvent, and reimagine the gospel," it might be more accurate to say of Lewis that he claims the gospel reforms or reimagines us for the sake of our encounter with pop culture. Our surrender, in other words, is already in the form of Jesus.

11. Ibid., 32.

12. Ibid., 142.

13. Ibid., 152–53.

14. Ibid., 10. It might be better to say that they simply do not acknowledge the way their own theological convictions are directly involved in their selection of pop culture materials with which to work. This unacknowledged means of making judgment is actually worse, since it depends on a kind of sophisticated connoisseurship of the gospel and culture they have developed in their lives but do not acknowledge or offer means to develop. Ironically, this is exactly what C. S. Lewis does offer!

15. See William Romanowski and Jennifer Vander Heide, "Easier Said than Done: On Reversing the Hermeneutical Flow in the Theology and Film Dialogue," *Journal of Communication and Religion* 30 (March 2007): 40–64.

16. In a section of his magisterial book *A Secular Age*, 171–74, Charles Taylor unpacks what he means by the term "social imaginary" as the way

ordinary people understand their social surrounds, a term he clarifies by describing what contemporary philosophers call "background." "It is in fact that largely unstructured and inarticulate understanding of our whole situation, within which particular features of our world show up for us in the sense they have." We might, I argue below, suspend judgment, but our presuppositions, our "background," we have with us always.

17. I don't mean to simply say the lyrics, separate from the music, offer meaning. In fact, the music is an integral aspect of the work and communicates on multiple levels of meaning. Yet the lyrics seem to be the main "content" suggested as relevant in Detweiler and Taylor's approach. More on these issues below.

18. Ludwig Wittgenstein, *Culture and Value*, trans. Peter Winch (Chicago: University of Chicago Press, 1980).

19. Rather than enter the scholarly debates that seek to define "popular" over against "high" culture, I first lead with the simple idea that popular culture is what lots of people like. If the record sells millions, it ought to raise the question, why?

20. Paul Holmer was Noah Porter Professor of Philosophical Theology at Yale and specialized in Kierkegaard and Wittgenstein. He found fascinating affinities between Lewis's and Wittgenstein's work. *C. S. Lewis: The Shape of His Faith and Thought* (New York: Harper and Row, 1976).

21. The story of their relationship is well told many places, including in a biography of great help to me, Alan Jacobs's *The Narnian: The Life and Imagination of C. S. Lewis* (New York: HarperCollins, 2005), esp. 269–79. The story is heartwarmingly told in the feature-length film *Shadowlands* (1993), directed by Richard Attenborough.

22. C. S. Lewis, *Letters to Malcom: Chiefly on Prayer* (New York: Harcourt, 1964), 44.

23. Ibid., 92.

24. Ibid, 93.

25. Holmer, *C. S. Lewis*, 20.

26. C. S. Lewis, *The Lion, The Witch and the Wardrobe* (New York: Harper, 1950), 48–49.

27. Holmer, *C. S. Lewis*, 34–35.

28. David Rozema, "'Belief' in the Writing of C. S. Lewis," in *C. S. Lewis as Philosopher: Truth, Goodness and Beauty*, ed. David Baggett, Gary Habermas, and Jerry L. Walls (Downers Grove, IL: InterVarsity, 2008), 156.

29. C. S. Lewis, *The Magician's Nephew* (New York: Harper and Row, 1955), 125.

30. Holmer, *C. S. Lewis*, 63–64.

31. Jacobs, *Narnian*, 294–95.

32. Lewis, *Experiment in Criticism*, 124.

33. Jacobs, *Narnian*, 294.

34. Lewis, *Letters to Malcom*, 92.

35. On this point my framing of the theological language has been influenced by my colleague Andrew Root's notion of place-sharing, drawn from his reading of the theology of the cross in Dietrich Bonhoeffer. See *Revisiting Relational Youth Ministry* (Downers Grove, IL: InterVarsity, 2007).

36. Lewis, *Experiment in Criticism*, 16–17.

37. Ibid., 18.

38. Ibid., 19–20.

39. Ibid., 22.

40. Ibid., 24.

41. Ibid., 25.

42. Ibid., 85.

43. Matt Jenson, *The Gravity of Sin: Augustine, Luther and Barth on homo incurvatus in se* (New York: Continuum, 2006).

44. Lewis, "Bulverism," in *God in the Dock: Essays on Theology and Ethics* (Grand Rapids: Eerdmans, 1994), 71.

45. I am thinking with and from Holmer's exposition in *C. S. Lewis*, 88–89.

46. Ibid., 108.

47. Lewis, *Experiment in Criticism*, 92.

48. Ibid., 94.

49. Ibid., 106.

50. Holmer, *C. S. Lewis*, 42.

51. Lewis, *Experiment in Criticism*, 115–16.

52. Ibid., 116–17.

53. Holmer, *C. S. Lewis*, 43.

54. Lewis, *Experiment in Criticism*, 121.

55. Ibid., 128.

56. The video is simply stunning and won music video of the year at the Video Music Awards (2005). Director Chris Milk said in an interview, "The message of the song, which becomes the subtext of the video, is that Jesus walks with everyone. Sinner, saint, murderer, drug dealer, it doesn't matter." See www.mvwire.com/2004/09/15/director-chris-milk-kanye-west-jesus-walks-music-video.

57. Jacob Bryant's powerful "Jesus Walks with Me? Kanye West's *The College Dropout*," published on the Web journal *The Ooze* gets at these issues brilliantly. See www.hcs.harvard.edu/~ichthus/issues/1.2/books_arts_bryant.html.

58. Josh Tyrangiel, "Why You Can't Ignore Kanye," *Time*, August 21, 2005. See www.time.com/time/magazine/article/0,9171,1096499,00.html.

59. Lewis, *Experiment in Criticism*, 116.

60. Ibid., 138.

61. The truth is that the best of human religion sees itself as overly important and indeed capable of influencing human and divine events. Gerhard Forde, *On Being a Theologian of the Cross* (Minneapolis: Fortress, 1997), 2.

62. Lewis, *Experiment in Criticism*, 138.

63. Ibid.

64. Ibid, 138–39.

65. Rowan Williams, *The Wound of Knowledge*, 2nd ed. (Boston: Cowley, 2003), 15.

66. Ibid.

67. Ibid., 17.

68. Ibid., 18.

69. Ibid., 19.

70. See here Dirk Lange, *Trauma Recalled: Liturgy, Disruption, and Theology* (Minneapolis: Fortress, 2010).

71. Martin Luther, *Luther's Works*, vol. 26, *Lectures on Galatians (1535)*, trans. and ed. Jaroslav Pelikan (St. Louis: Concordia, 1963), 350.

72. Lewis, *Experiment in Criticism*, 141.

Chapter 7 Practicing Surrender

1. Charlie Peacock, *At The Crossroads: An Insider's Look at the Past, Present and Future of Contemporary Christian Music* (Nashville: Broadman and Holman, 1999), 3.

2. Ibid., 17. The quote is from Rick Anderson, music buyer for a large chain of Christian stores.

3. Andy Crouch, *Culture Making: Recovering Our Creative Calling* (Downers Grove, IL: InterVarsity, 2008), 80.

4. Ibid., 89.

5. The *Saw* movies come up in chap. 5 as an example for the question to Adam Holz of *Plugged In* about reviewing R-rated movies. There have been seven movies in this series, beginning in 2004, always released the Friday before Halloween. See http://en.wikipedia.org/wiki/Saw_(franchise).

6. Dan Kimball, *Emerging Worship* (Grand Rapids: Zondervan, 2004), 14.

7. Meredith Whitmore, in *Plugged In*'s review of *American Idol* alumnus Jason Castro's cover of "Hallelujah." See www.pluggedin.com/music/albums/2010/jasoncastro-jasoncastro.aspx.

8. Neil McCormick, "Leonard Cohen: Hallelujah!" in *The Telegraph*, June 14, 2008, www.telegraph.co.uk/culture/music/3554289/Leonard-Cohen-Hallelujah.html.

9. On a Chicago radio show a few years ago, Larry "remarked that music rarely grabs him and takes him somewhere else, but when he heard Arcade Fire's album *Funeral*, it gave him hope that people were still out there making challenging music. See http://www.u2gigs.com/article410.html.

10. See www.tinariwen.com; also Barney Hoskyns, "Desert Blues: Tinariwen in the Raw," www.emusic.com/features/spotlight/294_200708.html.

11. Omar Sacirbey, "The 'Bono' of the Muslim World" on Beliefnet at www.beliefnet.com/Faiths/Islam/2006/01/The-Bono-Of-The-Muslim-World.aspx.

12. Ani Vrabel, "Harry Potter and the Supposed Allegiance with the Devil," *Paste*, July 14, 2009, www.pastemagazine.com/articles/2009/07/harry-potter-religion.html.

13. C. S. Lewis, *An Experiment in Criticism* (Cambridge: Cambridge University Press, 1961), 116.

14. Allison Graff, "Faith and Music, Calvin Style," www.calvin.edu/news/2008-09/ffm/.

15. Ibid.

16. This didn't stop Heffner and Calvin from being caught up in a "checklist Christianity" trap when in response to a huge wave of complaints, an invitation to the Canadian indie rock band the New Pornographers was rescinded. Heffner said, "For some people, the name, it hurts them, it confuses them. They wonder why would we ever associate the college with that word." See Troy Reimink, "Breaking Down Why Calvin College Canceled New Pornographers Concert: Can a Band's Name Be More Offensive than Its Music?" *Grand Rapids Press* (September 15, 2010), www.mlive.com/entertainment/grand-rapids/index.ssf/2010/09/pulling_the_plug_on_the_new_po.html.

17. Philip Pullman et al., *Darkness Illuminated: Platform Discussions on His Dark Materials at the National Theatre* (London: Oberon Books, 2004), 93.

18. Alan Jacobs, "The Youngest Brother's Tale: Harry Potter's Grand Finale," in *Books & Culture*, September 2007, www.booksandculture.com/articles/2007/sepoct/1.47.html.

19. Rowan Williams has spoken in just this way. Seeking to understand prayer, healing, and the power of God we often speak of personified in angels. See Rowan Williams, *Tokens of Trust: An Introduction to Christian Belief* (Louisville: Westminster John Knox, 2010), 48–52.

20. Ibid.

21. Luke Bell, *Baptizing Harry Potter: A Christian Reading of J. K. Rowling* (Mahwah, NJ: HiddenSpring, 2010), 4.

22. Ibid.

23. http://www.facebook.com/group.php?gid=2366633221.

24. http://www.facebook.com/group.php?gid=2243882733.

25. Andy Greenwald review, Eighteen Seconds before Sunrise, www.sigur-ros.co.uk/media/svefn/spin1.php.

26. John Best and Nick Abrahams, *Takk* interview and film, www.sigur-ros.co.uk/band/disco/takk-documentary.php.

27. Andrew, "Re:mote Induction–Sigur Ros Interview," http://rem_ind.tripod.com/audio/sigurint.htm.

28. "Sigur Rós: Why We're Mesmerised by the Hypnotic Iceland Band," *Independent,* January 20, 2009, www.independent.co.uk/arts-entertainment/music/features/sigur-r243s-why-were-mesmerised-by-the-hypnotic-icelandic-band-1519898.html.

29. Ibid.

30. Jessica Misener, "The Spiritual Side of Sigur Rós' Jonsi," in *Relevant*, www.relevantmagazine.com/culture/music/features/21039-the-spiritual-side-of-sigur-ros-jonsi.

31. www.blainehogan.com/post/352885169/an-act-of-confession.

32. www.sigur-ros.co.uk/news/?p=1589.

33. Steve Smith, "To Boldly Go Beyond the Limits of Sacred Music," *New York Times*, November 16, 2010, www.nytimes.com/2010/11/17/arts/music/17white.html.

34. Misener, "Spiritual Side."

35. *Paste* magazine listed *Funeral* as the number-three album on a top-fifty albums of the decade list here: http://www.pastemagazine.com/blogs/lists/2009/11/the-best-albums-of-the-decade.html?p=5.

36. Michael Barclay, "The Arcade Fire: Talk About the Passion," Exclaim.ca, September 2004, http://exclaim.ca/Features/OnTheCover/arcade_fire-talk_about_passion.

37. Ibid.

38. While various websites offer information about this former church (*petite église* means "little church"), this one offers photos for the curious: www.tout-sur-google-earth.com/t11398-street-view-eglise-transformee-en-studio-d-enregistrement.

39. Paul Morley, "Keep the Faith," *Guardian*, March 18, 2007, www.guardian.co.uk/music/2007/mar/18/popandrock.features11.

40. Sean Michaels, "Inside the Church of Arcade Fire," *Paste*, April 11, 2007, www.pastemagazine.com/action/article/4047/arcade_fire.

41. Ibid.

42. The church is a popular concert venue and has a beautiful Casavant organ. See http://lestjeanbaptiste.com/services-mission-culturelle/les-orgues-casavants-du-st-jean-baptiste/.

43. Typical of arguments of this sort, Thomas E. Ricks who serves as Pentagon correspondent for the *Washington Post* wrote the widely praised book *Fiasco: The American Military Adventure in Iraq* (New York: Penguin, 2006).

44. Michaels, "Inside the Church of Arcade Fire."

45. Morley, "Keep the Faith."

46. Ibid.

47. Tom Doyle, "Giant Steps: Arcade Fire, Band of the Year" *Q*, January 2011, 90.

48. Ibid, 87.

SUBJECT INDEX

SCRIPTURE INDEX